$5⁰⁰
$5156

Maine

Minn.

N. H.

N.Y. 1

Northeast

Mass.
Conn. R. I.

Wisc.

Mich.

Penna. N. J.

Iowa 3

North Central

Md. Del.

Ohio

W. Va.

Va.

Ill. Ind.

Mo.

Ky.

N. C.

Tenn.

S. C.

Ark.

Southeast

Ala. 2 Ga.

Miss.

La.

Fla.

The Ford Treasury of
FAMOUS RECIPES
from
FAMOUS EATING PLACES

Compiled by
NANCY KENNEDY

ARTHUR LOUGEE
Art Director

The Ford Treasury of
FAVORITE RECIPES
from
FAMOUS EATING PLACES

SIMON AND SCHUSTER · NEW YORK

DEDICATED TO
THE FORD AND LINCOLN-MERCURY DEALERS
OF THE UNITED STATES
WHOSE INTEREST AND SUGGESTIONS
HAVE MADE THIS GUIDE POSSIBLE

Foreword

THIS is the revised edition of a book under the same title, which first appeared in 1950, made up of recipes which had appeared up to that time in the departments "Favorite Recipes of Famous Taverns" in the FORD TIMES and "Outstanding Restaurants" in the LINCOLN-MERCURY TIMES. Additional recipes published in these magazines subsequent to 1950 have just appeared in a companion book, Volume II.

As stated in the original edition, we hope this book may be useful to travelers who know from experience that exciting food in an unusual atmosphere is often the highlight of an interesting motor trip—and the compensation for a tiresome one. We hope also that it may be equally serviceable to stay-at-home gourmets who like to try their hands at emulating some of the world's best chefs in their own kitchens.

Probably no one book could cover adequately *all* the really good eating places in the country; this edition is merely an attempt to present a representative group, with considerable emphasis on location as serving the needs of the touring public. Meanwhile, the work goes on in our magazine departments; perhaps by 1985 we may be a little closer to our goal of a really complete list of America's fine restaurants.

Happy motoring and successful cooking!

Dearborn, Mich.
 FORD MOTOR COMPANY
 William D. Kennedy, Editor-in-Chief
 FORD TIMES and LINCOLN-MERCURY TIMES

Contents

NORTHEAST

SOUTHEAST

NORTH CENTRAL

SOUTH CENTRAL

WEST

15

INDEX

Tow Path House THIS restaurant occupies one of the many picturesque mule barns built along the old Lehigh Canal. In summer, guests are served on two outdoor terraces. Open noon to midnight every day, except Monday.

SWEETBREADS

2 fresh sweetbreads
1½ cups water
2 beef bouillon cubes
1 cup small whole mushroom caps
2 tablespoons butter
2 tablespoons flour
½ cup thick cream
Thyme and salt to taste

Soak the sweetbreads in cold water 30 minutes, after removing fat and membrane. Cut in small pieces. Drop these in boiling beef stock (made with bouillon cubes and water) and cook 5 minutes. Drain (saving the stock). Sauté mushrooms quickly in 2 tablespoons butter; remove. Leaving the remaining butter in pan, combine this with 2 tablespoons flour, thyme, and salt. Add beef stock slowly; boil 2 minutes. Add cream, sweetbreads, and mushrooms. Bring to boil and serve on toast.

Mechanic Street, at the Canal, New Hope, Pennsylvania **NORTHEAST**

1

Pocono Manor THIS year-round resort hotel high in the Pocono Mountains is only 100 miles from Philadelphia and New York. A golf course and stables are maintained, and a full program of exciting winter sports is featured. Dining rooms are open every day from 8:00 a.m. to 8:00 p.m.

SPAGHETTI SICILIENNE WITH CLAMS

1 pound spaghetti
30 cherrystone clams and liquid
1 large onion, sliced
6 fillets of anchovies
5 fresh tomatoes, chopped
2 green peppers, chopped
½ clove garlic
4 ounces tomato purée
Salt and pepper to taste

Sauté onion in oil until slightly brown; then add clams and anchovies and cook together 5 minutes. Mix in tomatoes and green pepper, together with garlic and tomato purée; continue to cook for 20 minutes. Season to taste. Cook spaghetti separately (1 pound for 5 servings).

NORTHEAST   *Pocono Manor (north of Stroudsburg), Pennsylvania*

Wendover Farms GERMAINE and Louis Changeux
are hosts at this estate, once the summer home of "Gentleman
Jim" Corbett. Breakfast (house guests only), lunch, and
dinner, except Monday. Overnight accommodations.

BONELESS BAKED CHICKEN

3 3-pound broilers, split and boned
7 ounces bread crumbs
11 ounces lukewarm water
1 medium Spanish onion, sliced
4 ounces rendered chicken fat
4 ounces fresh chicken livers
1 teaspoon chopped parsley
¼ ounce salt
Pinch of black pepper
Dash of thyme
Dash of basil
Dash of oregano

Combine bread crumbs and water in
mixing bowl and allow to stand for
10 minutes. Brown onion in fat, then
sauté chicken livers in it. Put onion
and liver through meat grinder and
mix with bread crumbs and seasonings. Place in refrigerator overnight.
Use as stuffing for boned broilers.
Form each chicken around dressing to
get a chicken-like shape. Lightly broil,
then bake 20 minutes. Serves 6.

State Highway 9, Wappingers Falls, New York **NORTHEAST**

Old Mill Inn

A REBUILT barn, this inn still stands beside the century-old gristmill from which it derived its name. It is open every day—except on Mondays that are not holidays—for lunch and dinner. Comfortable overnight accommodations are available.

NEW ENGLAND PECAN PIE

1 cup pecan pieces
2 tablespoons flour
½ cup sugar
3 eggs
½ cup soft butter
Dash of salt
1 cup light syrup
1 teaspoon vanilla
Unbaked pie shell

Whipped cream

Mix flour thoroughly with sugar. Beat eggs slightly; add butter, salt, sugar mixture, syrup, nuts, and vanilla. Mix well and pour into unbaked pie shell. Preheat oven and bake for 10 minutes at 375° and for 50 minutes at 350°. Serve topped with whipped cream.

1

NORTHEAST

U.S. 202, Bernardsville, New Jersey

PAINTING BY GRANT REYNARD

The William Pitt

THIS popular eating place was named for that great benefactor of the early colonies, William Pitt, Earl of Chatham. It is open every weekday except Monday, from noon until 8:00 p.m., and Sundays from noon to 6:00 p.m.

COCONUT CREAM CHIFFON PIE

¾ cup shredded coconut
1 tablespoon gelatin
¼ cup cold water
3 eggs, separated
½ cup sugar
¼ teaspoon salt
1 teaspoon vanilla
1 cup scalded milk
2 cups heavy cream, whipped
1 baked pie crust

Sprinkle gelatin in cold water. Combine egg yolks, sugar, salt, and vanilla. Add to hot milk. Cook in double boiler until mixture coats spoon. Add gelatin to hot mixture; stir until dissolved. Chill until syrupy. Fold in stiffly beaten egg whites and 1 cup whipped cream. Pour into crust-lined pan and chill. Top pie with remainder of whipped cream and sprinkle with coconut.

94 Main Street, Chatham, New Jersey

NORTHEAST

1

Sportsman's Tavern   HARRY KAYE, once with the Stork Club, and Sampson Bowers, a native of Cooperstown, combined their talents to create this distinctive restaurant in a century-old farmhouse. Here excellent food is served in a restful atmosphere. Open from 8:00 a.m. to 1:00 a.m. daily.

STEAK TARTAR (one serving)

½ pound ground tenderloin
  of beef
1 egg yolk
1 tablespoon chopped raw onion
¼ teaspoon capers
2 anchovies
½ teaspoon English mustard
1 tablespoon Worcestershire sauce
1 tablespoon A-1 Sauce
1 tablespoon olive oil
Dash of hot sauce
Salt and pepper to taste

Mix ingredients together thoroughly. Form into a patty and place on plate. Garnish with teaspoon of chopped onions and chopped hard-boiled egg. Makes one serving. (If your cave-man instincts are dull, try cooking it!)

NORTHEAST   *On State Highway 28, 3 mi. west of Cooperstown, N. Y.*

Colligan's Stockton Inn

THE wishing well in the Inn's outdoor dining garden inspired the Rodgers and Hart melody "There's a Small Hotel with a Wishing Well." The Inn is open every day in the summer for dinner and supper. From Labor Day until June it is open every day, except Monday, from 5:00 p.m. till midnight.

TERRAPIN A LA COLLIGAN

1 quart terrapin meat
1 tablespoon dry mustard
½ pound butter
1 quart milk
  Salt and pepper to taste
  Pinch of cayenne pepper
1 jigger sherry

Heat terrapin and mustard in pan with a little butter; add milk and let come to a boil. Stir in remaining butter with salt and pepper. Add sherry at the last; then remove mixture immediately from heat and serve.

Bridge and Main Streets, Stockton, New Jersey

NORTHEAST 1

The River House BOATING on the Delaware has changed since George Washington's day. Among the pleasant additions are open-air dining patios, such as the one at the River House, perched on the river bank. It is open every day for lunch and dinner. Overnight accommodations.

TURKEY STEAK

> 1 turkey breast
> 1 quart milk
> 8 eggs
> Salt and pepper
> Flour
> Bread crumbs
> Deep fat
> Onion rings

Parboil a turkey of 25 to 26 pounds until fairly well done. Lift out breast and cut steaks as from a beef tenderloin. Dip steaks in a batter made of milk, eggs, salt, and pepper. Dredge in flour; then dunk back into batter and finish off with bread crumbs. Fry in fat (350°) until golden brown. Serve with onion rings made in same way.

1

NORTHEAST

South River Road, New Hope, Pennsylvania

PAINTING BY NORMAN G. RUDOLPH

Stevens House

THE Amish lend the dominant note to the local color of Lancaster County, but this inn is a part of the little-publicized English heritage of the region. The main dining room is a replica of Old London's Strand. A European plan hotel, with dining rooms open every day for breakfast, lunch, and dinner.

ROAST DUCK STUFFING

1½ loaves bread, cubed
2 large Spanish onions, chopped
1 large stalk celery, chopped
⅛ pound butter
1 egg
Sweet marjoram

Sauté the bread, onions, and celery together in the butter. Stir in the egg. Season to taste with the marjoram. Stuff the ducks (birds between 5 and 6 pounds and not more than six weeks old), and roast at an even temperature in a 350° oven. Quarter before serving.

South Prince and West King Streets, Lancaster, Pennsylvania **NORTHEAST**

1

25

Old Original Bookbinder's CLOSE enough
to the docks for a lively lobster to walk into the kitchen under his own power, this sea-food house has been famous since 1865. Open every day for lunch and dinner, except Sunday during July and August.

LOBSTER NEWBURG A LA BOOKBINDER

2 Maine lobsters
2 tablespoons butter
    Salt, pepper, paprika
3 egg yolks
¼ cup sherry
1 tablespoon flour
1 cup milk

Prepare sauce by melting butter over gentle flame and adding salt, pepper, and paprika. Stir in egg yolks and mix with sherry. Add flour and milk, and cook over low flame for 10 minutes. Steam lobsters—the Bookbinder method preserves tasty natural juices—then cut meat into small pieces and blend with sauce. Heat for 2 minutes. Place on thin toast and serve with fresh asparagus and new potatoes.

Shartlesville Hotel

Shartlesville Hotel PATRONS of this country hotel come miles to eat their way through stupendous Pennsylvania Dutch dinners. Continuous serving of country-style meals every day from 11:00 a.m. to 7:30 p.m.

FASTNACHTS

2 cups milk
1 yeast cake
1 cup warm water
6½ cups flour, approx.
1 cup sugar
3 eggs
½ teaspoon nutmeg
¼ cup melted butter
¼ teaspoon salt
Deep fat

Scald milk and set aside to cool. Dissolve yeast in water and add ½ cup flour and mix to a batter. Add the scalded milk and, when mixture is lukewarm, stir in 1 teaspoon sugar and about 3 cups flour. Set in a warm place to rise overnight. In morning add eggs, well beaten, nutmeg, butter, sugar, salt. Mix thoroughly. Stir in flour until batter can't be stirred with a spoon. Set aside to rise until light. Roll on a well-floured board and cut with a doughnut cutter. Let rise again and then fry in hot fat until golden brown.

State Highway 22, Shartlesville, Pennsylvania

NORTHEAST

1

Water Wheel Inn

BUILT in 1714, this building was a gristmill which ground corn and wheat for the Army during the Revolution. Now it's a restful spot for a quiet meal. The dining room is open for lunch and dinner every day until midnight, except Monday.

SAUERBRATEN

2½ pound round roast
⅔ cup water
⅓ cup cider vinegar
   Mixed spices
2 onions
2 carrots
2 celery stalks
   Gingersnaps

Pickle beef for three days in water and vinegar mixture. Add spices, chopped onions, carrots, and celery. Roast as regular pot roast. When meat is done make gravy from juice and vegetable mixture, thickening it with gingersnaps. At the Water Wheel this dish is served with noodles, potato dumplings, and red cabbage, making a real Pennsylvania Dutch dinner. Serves 5.

1

Old U. S. 611, Doylestown, Pennsylvania

Tarello's Restaurant

Six or eight times a year the gay window displays are changed here, but all year round it remains the "Home of Good Food." This fine restaurant, which is in the center of the business district, is open for lunch and dinner, except Saturday during July and August.

SPAGHETTI A LA RUSTICA

1 pound spaghetti
2 cloves garlic
Few sprigs parsley
¼ cup of olive oil
6 tomatoes
Salt and pepper
Grated Parmesan cheese

Chop garlic and parsley very fine, and cook with oil. When well browned, add cut tomatoes, salt, pepper. Continue cooking for about 40 minutes. Pour sauce over cooked spaghetti. Sprinkle with grated Parmesan cheese. Serves 4 to 6 persons.

1623 Chestnut Street, Philadelphia, Pennsylvania

Ye Olde Chop House

THESE wood-paneled walls should be well informed on financial matters, for they have overheard the secrets of Wall Street men for generations —ever since 1800. Lunch and dinner served from 11:30 a.m. to 7:30 p.m., except Monday and Friday.

CORNED BEEF AND CABBAGE

3½ pounds brisket of corned beef
2 onions
2 carrots
Celery leaves
1 head cabbage
Bacon rind or ham bone
2 teaspoons salt
Dash of pepper
4 tablespoons butter

Simmer beef slowly for 3 hours in water to which spices, 1 onion, carrots, and celery leaves have been added. Boil cabbage in fresh water with bacon rind or ham bone. Flavor with an onion, salt, and pepper. Cook until soft, about 20 minutes, and drain. Brown butter and pour over cabbage. Serve with corned beef. Makes 4 or 5 portions.

118 Cedar Street, New York, New York

Town and Country

THERE'S a choice here for every taste! The country kitchen turns out such hearty fare as pot roast of beef Pennsylvania, in contrast to lobster in sherry and cream, a specialty of the town kitchen. Open for lunch and dinner every day. Reservations advisable.

MAINE BLUEBERRY GRIDDLE CAKES

2 eggs
2 cups buttermilk
1 teaspoon soda
2 cups all-purpose flour
2 teaspoons baking powder
1 teaspoon salt
2 teaspoons sugar
4 tablespoons melted butter
1 cup fresh blueberries or frozen blueberries, thawed and drained

Beat eggs and add buttermilk mixed with soda. Sift flour, baking powder, salt, and sugar into this mixture; then pour in melted butter. Fold blueberries into batter, and fry on a hot griddle. Serve with maple syrup and sausage and you have the perfect breakfast for cold winter mornings.

284 Park Avenue, New York, New York

Tavern-on-the-Green

A setting in the midst of Central Park lends this urban restaurant the atmosphere of a country inn. Outdoor dining and dancing in spring and summer are added attractions. Open every day (except Mondays in winter) for dinner. Brunch on Sunday starts at 1:00 p.m.

TAVERN CHESTNUT DRESSING

1 pound chestnuts, chopped
½ loaf white bread
3 cups water
½ cup chopped Virginia ham
½ stalk celery, chopped
2 medium onions, chopped
1 tablespoon parsley

Soak bread in 3 cups water. Add chopped ham. Brown celery and onions lightly; add bread and ham together with chestnuts, freshly boiled. Stir thoroughly. Bake at 300°F. for 15 minutes. Serve with your holiday turkey which has been roasted separately after having been stuffed with a stalk of celery and chopped onions and carrots. Top with parsley.

PAINTING BY JOHN WEDDA

Hampshire House   ONE of the Kirkeby Hotels, this is famous both for its Dorothy Draper interior decorations and its continental cuisine. Overnight accommodations. Open all year for breakfast, lunch, and dinner.

VEAL STEAK SAUTE PROVENCALE

2—6-ounce veal steaks
Flour
4 ounces olive oil or butter
4 large mushrooms
1 clove garlic, crushed
6 ounces dry white wine
2 tomatoes, peeled and crushed

Roll steaks in flour and fry in olive oil or butter until brown on both sides; then remove from pan. Slice mushrooms into olive oil and fry 2 minutes before adding crushed clove of garlic. Fry another minute, then pour in wine and simmer until it is absorbed. Stir tomatoes into mixture before adding veal. Simmer 10 minutes. Serves 2.

150 Central Park South, New York, New York   **NORTHEAST**

Waldorf-Astoria

WHEN the Hotel Waldorf opened in 1893, it set the pace for elegance. Today dining rooms like the Starlight Roof carry on this tradition. Breakfast, lunch, dinner daily. Reservations advisable.

ICE CREAM PRALINE

1 pint cream
6 ounces granulated sugar
8 egg yolks
8 ounces praline paste
1 pint whipped cream
Fresh strawberries

Mix cream with the sugar and egg yolks; stir while cooking. Remove from fire before mixture boils, and cool. Then add praline paste, previously prepared by cooking together to the caramel point equal quantities of almond nuts and sugar which are cooled and reduced to paste. Strain the mixture; add whipped cream and set in a paper-collared mould and freeze for 1½ hours. Remove paper and serve on fancy ice form. Have very ripe fresh strawberries already macerated in "Cordial Medoc Liqueur" or good orange liqueur. Serve as a garnish.

NORTHEAST   *Park and Lexington Avenues, New York, New York*

1

Gage and Tollner's THE good strong coffee here is a clue to the rugged masculine atmosphere that has been maintained in the 76-year history of this chop house. A few brave women ask to have their coffee diluted, but the regulars view such feminine innovations as sacrilegious. Open 11:00 a.m. to 9:00 p.m every day except Sunday and some holidays.

CRAB MEAT VIRGINIA

6 ounces crab meat, fresh
Maryland lump kind

3 tablespoons butter

1½ tablespoons fresh lemon juice

1 sprig parsley

1 wedge of lemon

Place crab meat evenly on shallow individual baker. Add butter and lemon juice and bake in 400° oven for 8 minutes, or until golden brown. Serve in original baking dish, garnished with parsley and lemon wedge. Serves 1.

372-4 Fulton Street, Brooklyn, New York

NORTHEAST

1

35

PAINTING BY STANLEY STAMATY

The Blue Spruce Inn

AN old colonial farmhouse, complete with hand-hewn shingles, was converted to make this inn. A popular spot in the winter is the Polo Bar, which carries out the polo theme with Paul Brown paintings. Open every day, except Monday, for lunch, dinner, and supper.

SHRIMP IN DILL

To 2 quarts boiling water, add 3 pounds fresh unshelled shrimp, 1 tablespoon salt, 1 bay leaf, 3 peppercorns, 1 teaspoon vinegar, 1 crushed clove of garlic. Simmer, covered, 10 minutes. Remove from fire and let stand 20 minutes. Strain, saving 2 cups liquid. Shell shrimp and serve surrounded with Dill Sauce.

DILL SAUCE

Make a cream sauce with 2 cups shrimp liquid and 4 tablespoons flour; stir till smooth. Reduce to half by cooking, 1 cup dry white wine. Add 6 minced shallots to wine; then add this mixture to cream sauce. Bring to boil, stirring. Strain; add 8 tablespoons finely chopped dill. Season with salt and sherry wine. Serve hot.

NORTHEAST   *1480 Northern Boulevard, Roslyn, L. I., New York*

The Maine Maid IF you're hungry for Maine's way of cooking, you'll enjoy your meals in a 1789 farmhouse, where Vivian Roberts, a Maine native, turns out such delicacies as clam chowder, fish cakes, and clam pies. Open for lunch and dinner every day, except Monday. Closed January to first week in March.

CLAM FRITTERS

1 pint soft clams
2 cups flour
2½ teaspoons baking powder
2 eggs
½ cup milk
Clam juice
½ teaspoon salt
¼ teaspoon pepper

Drain clams and chop fine. Combine flour and baking powder. Beat eggs; add milk and clam juice. Add this slowly to flour, mix well, then add clams. Season with salt and pepper. Drop from a spoon into hot fat (375°), and fry until golden brown. Serve while hot. Helps make a real New England supper or cold-weather breakfast.

State Highways 106-107, Jericho, L.I., New York

NORTHEAST
37

Dahlstrom's Green Tree Lodge A PATH

has been worn around the smorgasbord table in this restaurant by guests who must view the delicacies from every angle. Lunch and dinner served every day, except Tuesday, with smorgasbord. Open from noon until 9:00 p.m.

DANISH LIVER PASTE LOAF

1½ pounds pork liver
¾ pound pork fatback
1 large onion, minced
2 cups rich white sauce
4 eggs
2½ teaspoons salt
½ teaspoon pepper
4 ounces anchovy paste
Dash of mixed spices

Grind liver and pork separately 3 times, then together, adding the onion. Combine with the white sauce. Beat well; add eggs one at a time; then seasonings. Turn into a well-greased pan and set in a pan of water. Grease a piece of brown paper fitted to the pan and tie over the top. Bake about 2 hours or until firm in a moderate oven.

1

NORTHEAST   *93 West Jericho Turnpike, Huntington Station, L. I., N. Y.*

Leighton's Woodlands Lake Restaurant

THIS restaurant, near Washington Irving's home, offers you the opportunity to lose a few pounds after your meal. You can rent a pedal boat-for-two on the lake. Lunch, dinner, and late supper served from noon until 1:00 a.m., except Monday.

CURRIED MINCED CAPON

4-pound capon
2 tablespoons butter
1 small onion, chopped
4 tablespoons curry powder
2 tablespoons flour
4 or 5 cups stock
Black pepper, cayenne, and salt

Simmer capon until tender. When done, remove skin and bone. Cut meat in small pieces. Save stock for sauce.

Prepare the sauce in this way:

Melt butter in large iron skillet and brown onion slightly. Add curry powder, flour, and hot stock. Boil gently until it has the consistency of thick cream. Add capon and simmer until ready to serve. Pour over steamed rice mixed with chutney and buttered green peas.

Saw Mill River Parkway, Ardsley, New York

NORTHEAST

1

Emily Shaw's

THIS restaurant is not far from the heart of metropolitan New York, but the country-quiet atmosphere makes the bustle of the city seem hundreds of miles away. Open from noon to midnight every day except Monday. Reservations necessary.

FRENCH-FRIED DEVILED EGGS

Cut 6 hard-boiled eggs lengthwise and remove yolks. Season yolks to taste with Worcestershire sauce, mustard, salt, black pepper, oil, and vinegar. Pack back into whites and hold together with toothpicks. Dip eggs into 2 beaten egg yolks, then flour and bread crumbs. Fry in deep fat until golden brown. Drain eggs on brown paper to rid them of excess grease; remove toothpicks.

Serve these deviled eggs in creole sauce, or serve them on spinach or other cooked greens.

State Highway 137, Poundridge, New York

The Hastings House

The Hastings House A comfortable nineteenth-century home is the setting for this restful summer restaurant owned and operated by Clara Hastings. Open for lunch and dinner every day except Sunday; from July 1 to September 15. Reservations preferred.

DATE TORTE

- 2 eggs, well beaten
- 1 cup powdered sugar
- 1 cup chopped dates
- 1 cup chopped nut meats
- 1 teaspoon baking powder
- 2 tablespoons flour

Mix the above ingredients in the order listed and bake in a shallow pan (about 7 inches by 11) for 20 minutes in a moderate oven. When cold, crumble and serve with whipped cream. Ice cream or custard may be substituted for the whipped cream. The torte keeps well if the correct amount of flour is used.

Georgian Inn

SET in a beautifully landscaped 5-acre park, this restaurant is furnished with rare antiques. For over 30 years patrons have been raving about its clam bisque, Long Island duckling, deviled crab, and other delicacies. Open noon until 9 p.m. except Monday; open Friday until 2:00 a.m. and Saturday until 3:00 a.m.

DEVILED CRAB

2 pounds fresh lump crab meat
2 cups heavy cream sauce
1 teaspoon dry mustard
Juice of ½ lemon
3 hard-boiled eggs, chopped
Deep-sea scallop shells
Bread crumbs
Paprika
Butter

Stir together cream sauce and crab meat. Add the mustard, lemon juice, and the hard-boiled eggs. Fill the scallop shells with mixture and sprinkle with bread crumbs, paprika, and dabs of butter. Bake in a hot oven until slightly brown.

1

NORTHEAST *124 East Jericho Turnpike, Huntington, L. I., New York*

Old Drover's Inn THERE's hearty fare, such as cheese soup before your meal, at this old inn, once Lafayette's headquarters. Open lunch and dinner daily, May through October. Closed Wednesdays November through April. Overnight accommodations; reservations advisable week ends in summer.

CHEESE SOUP

6 ounces young cheddar, grated
6 ounces well-cured cheddar, grated
4 tablespoons butter
½ cup diced carrot
½ cup diced green pepper
½ cup minced onion
½ cup minced celery
⅓ cup flour
1 quart well-seasoned chicken stock

3 to 4 cups *fresh* milk
Salt and white pepper

Melt butter in double boiler top. Add vegetables. Braise till tender, not brown. Blend in flour. Cook 1 minute, stirring constantly. Add stock and cook; stir till thick. Add cheese; stir till it melts. Thin with milk to creamy consistency. Season with salt, pepper. Strain. Reheat in double boiler. Serve hot—or in warm weather, very cold. Makes 2 quarts.

State Highway 22, Dover Plains, New York

NORTHEAST

1

Memory Inn

THE recipe dates back many generations. The inn is open every day for all meals until 10:00 p.m. Recreation facilities; overnight accommodations.

MEMORY INN MINCEMEAT

4 pounds cooking apples
2 pounds lean boiled beef
½ pound suet, chilled
1 pound seeded raisins
1 pound seedless raisins
1½ pounds currants
⅓ pound ground citron
1 teaspoon salt
½ teaspoon pepper
1 teaspoon allspice
1 teaspoon mace
1 teaspoon ground cloves
1 teaspoon nutmeg

2 tablespoons cinnamon
1 pound brown sugar
1½ quarts cider
1 cup brandy
1 cup Madeira wine

Peel and chop apples and combine with chilled beef and suet, also chopped. Mix in other ingredients except 1 pint cider and the brandy and Madeira. Boil this cider down to a cup of liquid; then add to mixture. Heat mixture through over low flame, stirring constantly. Remove, cool, and add brandy and Madeira.

NORTHEAST   *U.S. Highway 9, 3 miles south of Poughkeepsie, New York*

Mirror Lake Inn
A full range of summer and winter sports is offered at this lakeshore vacation estate, where you may stay in the pleasantly rambling main building or in one of the cottages. Open for breakfast, lunch, and dinner.

ADIRONDACK FLAPJACKS

4 eggs, separated
2 tablespoons sugar
½ teaspoon salt
2 cups milk
4 tablespoons butter, melted
2 cups flour
2 teaspoons baking powder

Beat egg whites and yolks separately. Then beat together egg yolks, sugar, salt, milk, butter, flour, and baking powder. Add whites last. Pour out individual flapjacks on a hot griddle. Serve with melted butter, and hot maple syrup which has been boiled until thick. Top with whipped cream.

Nelson House

APPROPRIATELY enough, the latest addition to this hotel is the Regatta Room, gaily decorated with murals of past races on the Hudson. The hotel was the unofficial headquarters for the Poughkeepsie Regatta for many years. Breakfast, lunch, dinner, supper from 7:00 a.m. to 1:00 a.m.

MARINATED FRESH SHRIMP

    1 pound fresh shrimp
    4 tablespoons olive oil
    1 small can tomatoes, strained
    1 pinch thyme
      Chopped parsley
      Salt and pepper
      Cooked rice ring

Remove shells and black line from shrimp and wash well. Drain and sauté in olive oil. When shrimp turns pink, add strained tomatoes. Simmer until shrimp is tender and sauce has thickened. Add pinch of thyme and parsley, and season to taste with salt and pepper. Fill center of rice ring with shrimp mixture and serve immediately.

1

NORTHEAST

28-44 Market Street, Poughkeepsie, New York

The Bird and Bottle Inn THIS two-century-old inn, beautifully furnished with antiques, is open for lunch and dinner every day except Tuesdays.

BAKED CHICKEN BIRD AND BOTTLE

3 broiler chickens, split in half
2 tablespoons onion, chopped
3 tablespoons green bell peppers, chopped
2 tablespoons celery, chopped
  Garlic clove, chopped fine, mashed
3 tablespoons parsley, chopped
1 cup chopped oysters, drained
1 teaspoon salt
½ teaspoon ground black pepper
¼ teaspoon cayenne pepper
5 tablespoons butter

1 cup bread crumbs
½ cup oyster juice

Sauté vegetables, oysters, and seasoning in butter. When tender, remove from pan. Add crumbs, oyster juice. Place chickens in pan, skin side up, ½ teaspoon butter on each half. Add ½ cup water. Bake (375°) 20 minutes. Remove, turn over, and fill cavity, back of chicken, with heaping spoonful dressing. Sprinkle with crumbs, melted butter. Bake 15 minutes. Garnish with cranberry or lingonberry preserve.

U.S. 9 (9 miles north of Peekskill), Garrison, New York   **NORTHEAST**

1

PAINTING BY C. H. ROBERTS

The Spring House BECAUSE of its proximity to the old Erie Canal and Monroe Mineral Springs, this restaurant was famous over a century ago. It derives its name from the ballroom floor, which "springs" because of its construction with a double set of joists. Open for lunch and dinner noon to 9:00 p.m., except Monday. Reservations advisable.

ROAST LONG ISLAND DUCKLING

Wash, singe, and clean a 5-pound duck. Season inside and out with salt. Fill cavities with apple dressing (cubes of apples and raisins). Truss duck. Roast in an uncovered pan in a slow oven, allowing 20 to 30 minutes per pound. Add a pinch of thyme. Baste every 10 minutes with drippings, adding a little water if needed. Cook until tender. Thicken drippings with flour. Serve with currant jelly or apple sauce. At the Spring House guests like their duckling served with candied yams and fresh Brussels sprouts.

NORTHEAST

3001 Monroe Avenue, Rochester, New York

The Krebs

DIETERS beware! This restaurant has built a national reputation, not only on the quality of its family-style meals, but on the quantity offered. Remember to save room for dessert, such as shortcake with whipped cream. Dinner served from noon until 9:00 p.m., except Friday; reservations advisable. Closed November 1 to first week in May.

HAM WITH SHERRY-MAPLE GLAZE

Place a Swift's Premium Ham fat-side up on a rack in an open pan. Use no water. Bake half hams in slow oven (325°) about 22 minutes per pound. If ham is taken from refrigerator, increase cooking time about 5 minutes per pound. Drain fat from pan. Skin ham, score, and stud with cloves. Pour 1 cup sherry wine or fruit juice over ham and let stand 5 minutes; then cover with 1 cup maple syrup. Brown in hot oven (400°) for about 15 minutes, basting frequently. Strain sauce into service dish. Serve surrounded by hot spiced fruit.

39 West Genesee Street, Skaneateles, New York

NORTHEAST

1

Hugo's Restaurant

GERMAN dishes are a specialty at this spot which is owned by Hugo Vogt and managed by Richard Heilemann. Lunch and dinner served daily till 1:00 a.m. If you are on the Merritt Parkway, take the exit at Long Ridge Road or High Ridge Road.

POTATO DUMPLINGS

3½ cups mashed potatoes
¼ teaspoon nutmeg
1½ teaspoons salt
¼ teaspoon white pepper
2 egg yolks
½ cup flour
4 quarts boiling, salted water

Mix potatoes, nutmeg, salt, pepper, and egg yolks. Form into small balls 1½ inches in diameter; then roll in flour to keep the outside from sticking. Drop carefully into boiling, salted water. When the dumplings rise to the top, simmer for 25 minutes. Remove and serve. The dumplings are served here with German sauerbraten. Makes 6 portions.

NORTHEAST

50

475 Atlantic Street, Stamford, Connecticut

Dorlon's Shore House HERE's a real old-fashioned New England shore house where all the food is cooked over a coal fire. Open for lunch and dinner from noon to 10:00 p.m., except Tuesday. Open May through November 1.

LOBSTER THERMIDOR

5 cold lobsters (meat)
10 lobster shells
1 cup flour
2½ quarts milk
½ pound onions, chopped
3 green peppers, chopped
1 whole pimento, finely chopped
8 ounces chopped mushrooms
1 pound butter
6 egg yolks
1 pint light cream
4 ounces sherry

Hollandaise sauce
Parmesan cheese
Paprika

Mix flour, milk, onions, green pepper, pimento, and mushrooms, and sauté in butter and egg yolks. Whip cream and fold into sauté mixture; then add sherry and lobster meat cut into ½-inch pieces. Fill lobster shells and pour hollandaise sauce on top. Sprinkle with grated Parmesan cheese and paprika. Bake to a golden brown.

Dorlon's Point, Norwalk, Connecticut

NORTHEAST

The Red Barn AT home in a 100-year-old restored barn, this restaurant is popular the year round. In summer you'll enjoy a stroll in the gardens; but winter will probably find you in front of one of the fireplaces. Meals served from 11:30 a.m. until 9:00 p.m.; open Saturday till 10:00 p.m.

FROZEN LEMON PIE

 3 egg yolks
⅛ teaspoon salt
½ cup sugar
¼ cup fresh lemon juice
½ teaspoon grated lemon rind
 3 egg whites
 1 cup cream, whipped
¾ cup crushed vanilla wafers

Beat yolks, salt, and sugar in top of double boiler. Stir in lemon juice and grated rind; cook over hot, not boiling, water until mixture thickens and coats spoon. Remove from fire and chill. Beat egg whites until stiff, and fold in whipped cream and cooked mixture. Sprinkle half of the wafer crumbs in freezing tray, then pour in mixture. Top with remaining crumbs and freeze until firm. Serve in finger-length slices.

NORTHEAST   *Merritt Parkway (Exit 41), Westport, Connecticut*

Old Riverton Inn   THIS Inn has functioned since 1796, when it was a stagecoach stop. Plan to visit the original Hitchcock chair factory on the opposite river bank from the Inn. Overnight accommodations and vacation facilities. Lunch and dinner every day; breakfast served to house guests and fishermen only.

CORNED BEEF SUPPER SALAD

   3 cups ground corned beef
   1 package prepared aspic
   2 cups boiling water
   6 tablespoons mayonnaise
   ½ teaspoon Worcestershire Sauce
   4 hard-boiled eggs, chopped
   Shredded cabbage
   Marinated raw carrots

Add boiling water to aspic; cool in refrigerator. Add corned beef and other ingredients; pour into ring mold and allow to set. Turn out on platter and fill center with shredded cabbage and raw carrots which have been marinated in French dressing. Garnish with unpeeled, scored cucumbers. Serve with mayonnaise. Serves 6 to 8.

State Highway 20, Riverton, Connecticut

NORTHEAST

1

53

Westleigh Inn

JOSEPH HACK, JR., president of the Inn, is easily recognized around town by the license tag on his Mercury station wagon, which reads merely INN, and his four magnificent St. Bernards. This former private estate was turned into a restful country hostelry. Breakfast, lunch, and dinner served daily. Overnight accommodations; vacation facilities.

BROILED SWEETBREADS VIRGINIE

Parboil sweetbreads until they turn white; chill in cold water. Split sweetbreads, butter them, season with salt and pepper, and broil slowly under slow fire until three-quarters done. Place them in a sauté pan with a little additional butter and finish cooking in the oven. In the meantime heat slices of ham in the broiler and sauté some medium-sized mushrooms over a slow fire. Place ham on a slice of toast and cover with sweetbreads and mushrooms. Top with a sauce, made of the butter used in cooking the sweetbreads and of mushrooms, blended with a little lemon juice and freshly chopped parsley.

NORTHEAST

U.S. 25, Litchfield, Connecticut

Fox Hill OVER 200 acres of gardens and virgin forest surround this inn, where you can swim in the pool, play golf, or just relax and enjoy the incomparable French cuisine. Breakfast, lunch, and dinner served every day. Overnight accommodations and vacation facilities. Reservations preferred.

POULET SAUTE

1 roasting chicken
Flour
⅛ pound butter
1 teaspoon tarragon vinegar
1 cup chicken broth
6 anchovies, chopped
8 stalks parsley, chopped

Quarter chicken and dip in flour. Sauté in butter (12½ minutes); when golden brown add vinegar and chicken broth. When this mixture thickens, sprinkle anchovies and parsley into it and boil not more than 1 minute.

U.S. 7, Ridgefield, Connecticut

PAINTING BY DOM LUPO

Stonehenge THE owner of this inn was stationed in England during World War II near the original Stonehenge. Breakfast, lunch, dinner to 1:00 a.m., except Tuesdays in winter. Overnight, vacation facilities. Reservations necessary.

ROAST CORNISH GAME HEN ON WILD RICE

4 game hens
Bacon fat
1 small onion, chopped
1 tablespoon flour
4 ounces sherry wine
1 cup water
3 tablespoons sour cream
1 teaspoon chopped chives
½ pound wild rice
2 ounces butter

Brush game hens with bacon fat. Roast in 350° oven. When half done, about 25 minutes, add onion. For gravy, combine flour, wine, and water, and stir into juice in baking dish. Simmer 5 minutes; then strain. Add sour cream and chives. Cook rice in 2 quarts water. When cooked, drain and add butter. Serve birds on rice. Pour gravy over them at table. Serves 4.

1

NORTHEAST

56

U.S. 7, Ridgefield, Connecticut

Skipper's Dock PERCHED on the end of a wharf, this picturesque restaurant annually attracts thousands of visitors. Don't forget to visit the world-famous Marine Museum in nearby Mystic. Restaurant open from noon to 10:00 p.m., first of May to October 15. Reservations advisable.

SYLLABUB

1 angel cake
8 ounces heavy cream
3 heaping teaspoons sugar
3 ounces sherry
Maraschino cherries

Lightly whip heavy cream; add sugar and sherry wine. Mix thoroughly until sugar is dissolved. Spread this sauce generously over each slice of angel cake, covering top and sides completely. Decorate with halved maraschino cherry on top of outside corners. This delicious dessert is one of the Dock's many original dishes.

Front Street, Noank, Connecticut

NORTHEAST

1

Country Squire Inn

MOST people enjoy their summer meals served in the old woodshed here, despite possible unpleasant childhood associations. In the Inn's art gallery, well-known artists exhibit their work. Open for lunch and dinner except Monday; April 15 to Thanksgiving Day.

TURKEY KILLINGWORTH

Place cooked broccoli on the bottom of individual pie tins (one for each person to be served). Cover with sliced turkey; then cover with cheese sauce (see below) served piping hot from the broiler.

CHEESE SAUCE
½ pound American cheese
1 quart chicken stock

½ teaspoon dry mustard
4 tablespoons butter ⎱
4 tablespoons flour ⎰ make roux
Salt and pepper
Dash of Worcestershire Sauce

Add cheese and seasonings to stock and simmer in double boiler.

NORTHEAST

State Highway 80, Killingworth, Connecticut

Colonial Inn

THIS stately old inn heard the opening shots of the Revolution in 1775, and was used as a storehouse and aid station for the men who "fired the shot heard round the world." Overnight and vacation facilities. Breakfast, lunch, and dinner served every day.

COUNTRY BAKED BEEF PIE

1 pound stewing beef, cubed
Flour
½ tomato, chopped
2 small onions, chopped
1 small carrot, diced
Clove of garlic
Worcestershire Sauce
A-1 Sauce
Salt and pepper
Pastry crust

Dredge cubes of beef in flour and braise in the oven in an uncovered pan. Sauté tomato, onions, carrots, and clove of garlic in a skillet; add to the braised beef. Cover with water and stew until tender. Season to taste with Worcestershire Sauce, A-1 Sauce, salt, and pepper. Place in a pie dish and cover with pastry crust. Bake until brown. Serve piping hot.

11 Monument Square, Concord, Massachusetts

Towne Lyne House

A MAMMOTH glassed-in terrace overlooking Lake Suntaug gives diners here a changing scene with each season. Open for lunch and dinner, except Monday, the year round. Reservations advisable.

LOBSTER THERMIDOR

1¼ pounds hot boiled lobster
6 medium mushrooms, cooked
1 teaspoon chopped parsley
½ teaspoon paprika
¼ teaspoon dry mustard
⅛ teaspoon salt
Few grains pepper
½ teaspoon butter
Juice of ⅛ lemon
1 tablespoon sherry
½ cup cream sauce
1 tablespoon Parmesan cheese

Remove lobster meat from claws and body of lobster. Save shell to refill. Leave small claws on—they will help shell to stand upright. Cube meat and combine with mushrooms, chopped parsley, paprika, dry mustard, salt, pepper, and lemon juice, and sauté in melted butter. Then remove from the fire; add sherry and cream sauce (combine 1 cup cream, ¾ ounce flour, ¾ ounce butter). Refill lobster shell with mixture. Sprinkle with cheese and bake in moderate oven. Serves 1.

NORTHEAST *Newburyport Turnpike, Lynnfield, Massachusetts*

PAINTING BY LORING W. COLEMAN

The Wayside Inn

THE poet Longfellow, in *Tales of a Wayside Inn,* describes this as a "region of repose." In 1923 it was purchased by Henry Ford and furnished with rare antiques. Open for breakfast, lunch, tea, and dinner. Reservations preferred. Overnight accommodations.

NEW ENGLAND CLAM CHOWDER

1 quart clams, chopped, and juice
¼ pound salt pork, diced
2 medium onions, diced
3 cups diced raw potatoes
½ teaspoon salt
¼ teaspoon pepper
2 cups boiling water
1 quart milk

2 tablespoons butter
1 pint light cream

Cook pork until crisp, add onions, and cook 5 minutes. Mix in potatoes, seasonings, and water; cover pan and simmer for 10 to 15 minutes. Add clams and their liquor; then milk, butter, and cream. Heat and serve.

U. S. 20, South Sudbury, Massachusetts

The 1812 House

THIS lovely old colonial home, turned restaurant, is one of the famous Treadway chain. Meals are served from noon until 8:30 p.m. every day. Reservations advisable; open from April 1 to November 30.

1812 HOUSE CRAB MEAT PIE

1 cup crab meat or crab flakes
2 ounces butter
  Flour for roux
1 pint light cream, scalded
2 hard-boiled eggs
  White wine
  Dash of cayenne pepper
  Potato chips and crackers

To make cream sauce, melt butter in a saucepan and mix with a little flour. Add cream, stirring constantly, and cook till sauce is medium thick. Toss in crab meat and eggs, and a generous portion of white wine. Bring mixture to boil; then place in casserole. Top with potato chips and crackers. Dot with butter and bake until brown.

NORTHEAST   *11 Salem End Road, Framingham Center, Massachusetts*

The White Drum

THIS *non*-colonial, popular restaurant occupies an attractive modern building. Meals served from 11:30 a.m. to 9:00 p.m. Reservations advisable on Sunday. Open April 1 to December 1.

WHITE DRUM SALAD WITH TOMATO SOUP DRESSING

DRESSING

1 can Campbell's tomato soup
¾ cup vinegar
½ cup oil
¼ cup sugar
1 tablespoon Worcestershire Sauce
1 small onion, chopped
1 green pepper, chopped
1 teaspoon salt
1 teaspoon paprika

Combine ingredients and mix well. Pour desired amount on salad; keep remainder in refrigerator. Makes 1 quart.

SALAD

Combine the following: a head of lettuce broken into pieces, a sliced Chinese cabbage, an unpeeled cucumber cut in thick slices, tomatoes cut in wedges, sliced radishes, raw cauliflower broken into flowerets, sliced celery, and watercress. Place in a bowl rubbed with a clove of garlic and toss with dressing. Serves 6 to 8.

Intersection of State Highways 2 and 78, Orange, Mass.

NORTHEAST

Four High Road   THE first newspaper in town was published in this house, which was built in 1670. Open for lunch and dinner except Sunday and Monday. Reservations necessary for dinner. Open the first of March through November.

PINEAPPLE MINTFREEZE

½ cup crushed pineapple
½ cup sugar
½ cup water
½ teaspoon mint extract
   Green food coloring
½ cup lemon juice
1 cup ginger ale

Put sugar, water, mint, and food coloring in saucepan and simmer for 10 minutes. Add lemon juice, pineapple, and ginger ale, and pour into refrigerator tray. Freeze and serve either as a dinner sherbet or a refreshing dessert. Delicious also as a fruit salad topping.

4 High Road, Newbury, Massachusetts

1

NORTHEAST

Williams Inn

ON the elm-shaded campus of Williams College, this inn has built up a reputation for comfort combined with excellent food. Open the year round for breakfast, lunch, and dinner. Overnight accommodations and vacation facilities. Reservations preferred.

BOSTON BROWN BREAD

- 3 cups bread flour
- 3 cups yellow corn meal
- 3 cups whole wheat flour
- 1 tablespoon baking soda
- 2 cups raisins
- 1 tablespoon cinnamon
- 1 tablespoon ginger
- 3 eggs, beaten slightly
- 3 cups molasses
- 3 cups sour milk

Mix dry ingredients together first; then combine remaining items in a separate bowl. Add dry mix to this liquid and stir well. Spoon equal parts into 4 well-greased, tall No. 5 tins. Cover with lids or waxed paper tied on firmly and steam for 3 hours. Makes 4 loaves.

College Place, Williamstown, Massachusetts

NORTHEAST

1

PAINTING BY HARVEY KIDDER

The Old Mill   YANKEE ingenuity transformed an old sawmill into this popular restaurant. Open for breakfast, lunch, and dinner from 7:30 a.m. to 10:00 p.m., except Christmas Day. Reservations advisable week ends and holidays.

NEW ENGLAND BAKED BEANS

- 1½ cups dried beans, kidney or California pea
- 2 tablespoons chopped onion
- ¼ pound salt pork
- ⅓ cup molasses
- ¼ teaspoon mustard
- 1½ tablespoons brown sugar
- 2 tablespoons catsup
- 1 teaspoon salt
- ⅛ teaspoon pepper
- 1 tablespoon butter

Pick over beans and rinse with cold water. Cover with water and soak overnight. Drain and cover with fresh water; simmer about ½ hour until skins burst when blown on; drain. Together with chopped onion put in a greased bean pot with salt pork cut in chunks. Mix remaining ingredients with 2 cups hot water and pour over beans. Add enough water to cover beans; dot with butter. Cover pot and bake in slow oven about 6 hours. Add water as needed.

1

NORTHEAST

66

State Highway 2A, Westminster, Massachusetts

The Blacksmith Shop

A REAL old blacksmith's forge, where the chef broils native lobster, fish, and meats, is the center of interest at this harbor-front restaurant. Breakfast, lunch, and dinner are served, except Monday. Open May 15 to October 15.

FROZEN GINGER ALE SALAD

    1 tablespoon plain gelatin
    2 tablespoons cold water
    ¼ cup ginger ale, heated
    ¼ cup lemon juice
    1½ cups ginger ale, cold
    ¼ cup celery, chopped
    ½ cup seedless grapes
    ½ cup pineapple, crushed
    ½ cup preserved ginger, chopped
    Lettuce

Cream mayonnaise (½ whipped cream and ½ mayonnaise)

Soak gelatin in cold water; add heated ginger ale and dissolve. Stir in lemon juice and cold ginger ale. Place mixture in refrigerator to set. When it begins to stiffen, add celery and fruit. Return to refrigerator to set. Serve on high beds of lettuce cut square. Garnish with cream mayonnaise.

On the harbor front, Rockport (Cape Ann), Massachusetts

NORTHEAST 1

Hartwell Farm

THIS house was built in 1636 by William Hartwell, who came to Concord "because Boston was too crowded." Since 1925 it has been a restaurant. Open for lunch and dinner, except Monday. Reservations advisable. Closed month of January.

HARTWELL FARM BAKED HAM

Bone and tie one 15- or 16-pound smoked ham. Place in roasting pan with 2 cups cold water. Make a "blanket" for the ham by adding cold water to 8 cups flour until mixture has consistency of biscuit dough. Turn onto a well-floured board and knead as much flour as possible into the dough. Roll out to a thickness of ½ inch. (The dough will be tough and will not roll easily.) Place blanket of dough over the ham. Put a tight-fitting cover on the roasting pan. Bake in a 375° to 400° oven 3 hours. Then test ham with fork to make sure it's cooked. If done, remove from oven. Take off skin and cover with brown sugar. Poke cloves into fat. Return to oven, uncovered, till brown. Put on platter; cover with syrupy mixture from pan.

NORTHEAST *Virginia Road (off State Highway 2A), Concord, Mass.*

Brookfield Inn   MANY famous people have been entertained here; among them Calvin Coolidge and Franklin D. Roosevelt. Breakfast, lunch, dinner, and supper until 1:00 a.m. Overnight accommodations.

BROOKFIELD INN WINE SPONGES

> 6 eggs, separated
> 6 tablespoons sugar
> 6 tablespoons flour
> Grated rind of 1 lemon

Whip egg yolks; add sugar and mix thoroughly. Sift in flour and mix well. Fold in stiffly beaten egg whites, add lemon rind; then drop batter by teaspoonfuls into deep fat and fry until golden brown. Remove and let drain on brown paper. (They may be kept for several weeks in a tightly lidded jar.)

SAUCE

To 1 quart white wine or cider add a small stick of cinnamon, a few slices of lemon, and sugar to taste. Drop the little sponge cakes in the cold wine or cider and bring to a boil. Simmer slowly for a half hour. Serve hot.

State Highway 9, Brookfield, Massachusetts

NORTHEAST

69

Publick House A WONDERFUL restoration job has been performed on this 1771 inn. The original wide fireplaces and hand-hewn beams remain, but air conditioning and other modern improvements make it a more comfortable spot today than it was in George Washington's time. Open for breakfast, lunch, and dinner. A la carte until midnight in the cocktail lounge. Overnight accommodations. Reservations necessary.

INDIAN PUDDING

1 quart milk
3 ounces corn meal
3 eggs
4 ounces sugar
1 teaspoon vanilla
1 teaspoon cinnamon
1 teaspoon salt

½ pint molasses
Grated rind of one orange

Boil milk; add corn meal. Bring to boil and let cook for 5 minutes. Add remaining ingredients and bake for an hour.

NORTHEAST

Main Street, Sturbridge, Massachusetts

Wiggins' Old Tavern

THIS reproduction of an early American tavern is popular with Smith students and faculty as well as visitors to this pleasant college town. Open for breakfast, lunch, and dinner until 11:00 p.m. An adjoining hotel, the Hotel Northampton, under the same management, offers overnight accommodations and vacation facilities.

PECAN PIE

1¼ cups pecans
5 eggs
2 cups corn syrup
¼ cup molasses
⅛ pound butter, melted
1 teaspoon vanilla
Pinch of salt
1 pie shell, unbaked

Beat eggs well; add corn syrup, molasses, butter, vanilla, salt, and pecans. Fill a pie tin lined with a rich pie crust. Bake in medium oven for about 40 minutes.

36 King Street, Northampton, Massachusetts

NORTHEAST

Parker House

FOR over 98 years this hotel, in the shadow of historic King's Chapel, has been a haven for travelers. Here the Parker House rolls originated. Open for breakfast, lunch, and dinner daily.

BROILED SCROD A LA PARKER

9-ounce portion of fillet of scrod
Salt and pepper
Flour
Oil
Bread crumbs

Season the scrod with salt and pepper; dredge in flour, then oil, and lastly bread crumbs. Broil about 6 minutes on both sides, butter well, and serve with lemon and parsley. The recipe for this delicious and universally popular sea-food dish will serve one person. Suggested to be served with the scrod are parsley buttered potatoes and fresh new peas.

60 School Street at Tremont, Boston, Massachusetts

Union Oyster House   OPEN since 1826, this
famous sea-food restaurant still boasts its original stables and
oyster bar. Louis Philippe of France once lived here. Open
8:00 a.m. to 9:00 p.m. daily.

NEW ENGLAND CLAM CHOWDER

1 quart soft clams
¼ cup diced salt pork
3 small onions, sliced
4 cups diced potatoes
2 tablespoons flour
2 teaspoons salt
⅛ teaspoon pepper
2½ cups boiling water
1 quart milk, scalded
2 tablespoons butter

Separate clams from liquor, discard
dark stomach contents, and mince
clams. Fry pork to a golden brown,
then add sliced onions, and fry these
to a light golden color. Add a layer of
potatoes and sprinkle with flour, salt,
and pepper. Add clams, then another
layer of potatoes sprinkled with remainder of flour, and with salt and
pepper. Add boiling water and simmer
until potatoes are done. Combine milk,
clam liquor, and butter before adding
to clam mixture. Simmer for 5 minutes.
Serve with crackers.

41 Union Street, Boston, Massachusetts

NORTHEAST

Andover Inn THE original Inn was adapted from the home of Harriet Beecher Stowe and moved to its present location on the campus of Phillips Academy in 1930. Open for breakfast, lunch, and dinner. Overnight accommodations.

BAKED INDIVIDUAL LOBSTER PIE

1 cup buttered and seasoned
   bread crumbs
1¼-pound lobster, boiled and
   shelled
¼ cup lobster stock
¼ cup milk
¼ cup drawn butter

Cover bottom of individual casserole with the bread crumbs. Dice lobster meat into large pieces and put in casserole on top of crumbs. Cover with lobster stock and milk. Make a topping of the bread crumbs and bake until heated through and crumbs are a golden brown (15 minutes in a hot oven). Moisten completely with drawn butter after baking. Garnish with small lobster claws; place wedge of lemon on lettuce leaf.

1

NORTHEAST

Chapel Avenue, Andover, Massachusetts

PAINTING BY ALOIS FABRY, JR.

Old Chase House

HERE's a restful spot to spend your Cape Cod vacation or to enjoy a delicious meal. For over 240 years this house has stood here on the banks of the Little Herring River. Breakfast; lunch and dinner, noon to 10:30 p.m. Overnight accommodations, recreation facilities. Closed September 15 to June 15. Reservations preferred for dinner.

MERINGUES

2 egg whites
3 drops vinegar
½ teaspoon water
Pinch of salt
½ cup fine granulated sugar
½ teaspoon vanilla

Beat whites until stiff; add vinegar, water, and salt. Beat a little, then add sugar gradually, and finally add vanilla. Beat until stiff but not dry. Drop spoonfuls of meringue on greased cookie sheet and cook for 1 hour in 250° oven. Cool slowly. Serve filled with vanilla ice cream and topped with strawberry or chocolate sauce. Keep extras in airtight can.

State Highway 28, West Harwich, Cape Cod, Massachusetts **NORTHEAST**

1

General Glover Inn

ONCE the home of the Father of the American Navy, General John Glover, this house attracts gourmets with its good food. Open noon to 9:00 p.m.

EAST INDIA CURRY OF CHICKEN

4 pounds frying chicken, cut for serving

¼ cup vegetable oil or butter

2 medium-sized onions, chopped

1 minced clove of garlic (optional)

2 bay leaves

Several peppercorns

1 teaspoon paprika

2 teaspoons curry powder

Salt to taste

Pour butter or oil in heavy sauce pan, add onion, and cook until golden brown. Add chicken and rest of ingredients (except curry powder) and cook for about 10 minutes. Add enough boiling water to cover chicken and simmer till meat is tender. Add curry powder and simmer 5 minutes more. Thicken with flour and water. Remove chicken and arrange on a platter with a ring of boiled rice around it. Cover both rice and chicken with the curry sauce; garnish with French fried onions or toasted coconut. Serve with chutney. Makes 6 portions.

U. S. 1A, Swampscott, Massachusetts

Pine Wood Inn and *Cottages* Louis Holtz-
BERGER is a host in the Old World tradition at this pleasant
country inn. Breakfast, lunch, dinner. Overnight accommodations and vacation facilities. Open June 15 to September 15.

DUTCH OVEN ROAST

3- to 4-pound top round beef
3 tablespoons beef fat
1 onion, sliced
2 small carrots, coarsely chopped
¼ stalk celery, coarsely chopped
1 stalk leek, coarsely chopped
3 tablespoons flour
½ cup tomato purée
½ glass red wine
1½ quarts hot water or soup stock
3 cloves

1 bay leaf
Black pepper and salt

Heat beef fat in Dutch oven until
hot. Add meat. Turn meat until
browned all over; remove from pan.
Brown onion in beef fat before adding
other vegetables to be browned. Blend
flour and tomato purée into mixture.
Pour wine and water (or stock) into
Dutch oven. Boil a few minutes; then
return meat to pan. Add seasonings.
Cook slowly 2 to 2½ hours.

State Highway 11, New Durham, New Hampshire   **NORTHEAST**

Wentworth-by-the-Sea

A SALT-WATER swimming pool is one of the many recreational features of this historic resort hotel on its piny island in Little Harbor. Breakfast, lunch, and dinner served; overnight and vacation facilities. Open May 15 to October 1. Reservations necessary.

NEW HAMPSHIRE FRUIT COOKIES

1 cup butter
1½ cups sugar
3 eggs, well beaten
1½ tablespoons water
3¼ cups flour, sifted
1 teaspoon baking soda
¼ teaspoon salt
½ teaspoon cinnamon
½ cup raisins, chopped
½ cup currants, chopped
1 cup walnuts, chopped

Cream butter and sugar together until light and fluffy. Add eggs and water; beat thoroughly. Sift dry ingredients together and add to mixture with fruits and nuts. Mix well. Drop by teaspoonfuls on a greased cookie sheet and bake in 350° oven 15 minutes. Makes 48 cookies.

1

NORTHEAST

Portsmouth (Newcastle), New Hampshire

The Walpole Inn SINCE 1890 this inn has offered a comfortable vacation spot combined with truly imaginative food. Be sure to notice the water-color murals depicting local scenes. Open for breakfast, lunch, and dinner. Overnight accommodations and recreation facilities.

WALPOLE WOODCHUCK RELISH

1 medium cabbage, shredded
2 green peppers, cut julienne
2 sour pickles
2-ounce can pimentos
  Celery seed
  Garlic powder
  Olive oil
  Vinegar

Pepper
Salt
⅛ teaspoon sugar

Combine vegetables. Add celery seed, garlic powder, olive oil, vinegar, pepper, and salt to taste. Sprinkle sugar over relish. Delicious with meat.

State Highway 12, Walpole, New Hampshire

NORTHEAST

Peckett's-on-Sugar Hill

As THE name implies, this inn is located on the slope of Sugar Hill with an uninterrupted view of the White Mountains and Franconia Range. Breakfast, lunch, and dinner served. Overnight accommodations and vacation facilities. Open May 27 to October 15. Reservations preferred.

PECKETT'S CREAM-BAKED CHICKEN

1 broiler
Salt and pepper
Paprika
Flour
Butter
½ pint cream

Quarter the broiler and sprinkle with salt, pepper, and paprika. Dust chicken with a little flour. Sauté in butter until light brown on both sides. Place chicken in pan and cover with 1 cup hot water; let steam on top of stove until tender. Pour cream over chicken. Cover pan and cook slowly for 30 minutes. Remove cover and brown by sautéeing for 5 minutes before serving.

Franconia, New Hampshire

Windham County Hotel

HERE'S a unique hotel—one that handily has a jail attached. It all began when local city planners were overly optimistic about the growth of the town and built onto the lonely jail. The manager is both hotel host and jailer. Breakfast, lunch, and dinner served. Overnight accommodations (hotel or jail) and vacation facilities.

BANANA BREAD

3 very ripe bananas
¾ cup sugar
Pinch of salt
1 egg
¼ cup butter
1 teaspoon soda
1 tablespoon water
2 cups pastry flour

Mash bananas with a fork. Blend in sugar, salt, and beaten egg. Melt butter and stir into banana mixture. Dissolve soda in water and add with sifted flour. Mix and bake in loaf pan for 45 minutes in 350° oven. Makes 1 loaf.

State Highway 30, Newfane, Vermont

NORTHEAST

Barrows House THE main building of this resort
hotel is over 185 years old and was opened as an inn over a
half century ago. Breakfast, lunch, and dinner served. Open
May 15 to October 15. Reservations necessary.

LIME GELATIN AND COTTAGE CHEESE SALAD

2 packages lime gelatin
1 pint hot water
1 pint cold water
1 pint cottage cheese
    Crisp lettuce leaves
    Mayonnaise mixed with whipped
    cream

Dissolve gelatin in hot water; add
cold water and cool. When it starts to
set, add cottage cheese and beat with
egg beater. Pour into ring mold and
chill in refrigerator. Serve on lettuce
topped with mayonnaise mixture.
Makes 10 average-size salad portions.

State Highway 30, Dorset, Vermont

The Worster Hotel

THE roster of famous guests at this century-old hostelry is studded with names like Daniel Webster, President Franklin Pierce, and Oliver Wendell Holmes. Breakfast, lunch, and dinner served 11:30 a.m. to 8:00 p.m., except Saturday. Overnight accommodations.

YANKEE POT ROAST

4 pounds beef, bottom round
¼ pound salt pork, sliced
1 cup flour
1 teaspoon salt
¼ teaspoon black pepper
1 pint water

Fry out salt pork. Rub beef on all sides with mixture of flour, salt, and pepper. Remove pork and brown beef well on all sides in fat. Add water and cook in Dutch oven until beef is tender. Remove beef, thicken and season gravy.

Corner Winthrop and Second Streets, Hallowell, Maine   **NORTHEAST**

Sunset Farm The sundeck and patio here overlook the picturesque islands of Casco Bay and the distant White Mountains. Hot biscuits with homemade jams are a popular feature with every meal. Open from noon until 8:00 p.m. from May 1 to October 1. Reservations advisable.

SUNSET FARM PLUM RUM JAM

3½ cups plums, chopped fine
½ cup lemon juice
7½ cups sugar
½ bottle pectin
¼ cup good dark rum

Combine plums, lemon juice, and sugar in a kettle; boil hard for 3 minutes, stirring constantly. Then add pectin and rum; stir at intervals for 5 minutes. Pour into jam jars and seal.

1

NORTHEAST

Basin Point, South Harpswell, Maine

PAINTING BY F. W. SAUNDERS

Jordan Pond House

SURROUNDED by Acadia National Park, this restaurant has been serving tourists since 1894. Unique feature is the birch-bark paneling in the two dining rooms. Lunch, tea, and dinner served from noon to 8:00 p.m. Reservations necessary for breakfast. Open from last week in June through September.

PEACH ICE CREAM

1 heaping 2-quart basket peaches
5½ cups sugar
½ teaspoon salt
⅓ cup lemon juice
3½ quarts heavy cream

Peel and pit peaches, then grind. Add sugar, salt, lemon juice, and cream. Freeze as you would regular ice cream. If your family is small, halve the recipe but don't underestimate anyone's capacity for this delicious summer treat.

Jordan Pond Road, Seal Harbor, Maine

Château Frontenac

ONE of the most luxurious hotels in Canada, the Château is built on a hill overlooking the city. Overnight accommodations. Breakfast, lunch, and dinner.

BOUILLABAISSE A LA MARSEILLAISE

¼ pound chopped onions
2 leeks (white part only), squared
3 ripe tomatoes, peeled
1 clove garlic, crushed
1 teaspoon chopped parsley
1 pinch saffron
½ cup olive oil
1 bay leaf

1 pound wall-eyed pike, boned and cut in squares
1 pound sole, boned and cut in squares
1 pound haddock, boned and cut in squares
2 dozen oysters
½ pound shrimps
Salt and pepper

Place this mixture in a frying pan and fry for about 5 minutes, then add:

1 live lobster, cut in chunks

Cover ingredients with water. Cook 20 minutes. Serve hot in casserole surrounded with dried French toast.

NORTHEAST

Quebec City, Quebec

Green Shutters IN this old inn the Dutch ovens and fireplaces remain. Overnight accommodations and vacation facilities. Meals served to guests or by special arrangement. Reservations preferred. Open May 1 to November 15.

FISH CHOWDER

2½-pound fish (halibut, cod, or haddock)
2 ounces salt fat pork
1 large onion
2 medium-size potatoes
1 quart milk or cream
6 crackers
Salt and pepper

Dice pork, onion, and potatoes. Boil fish in small amount of water until nearly separated from the bones. Remove skin and bones; break up any large pieces of fish. Save water. Fry pork in soup pot until cubes are a delicate brown. Add onion, potatoes, and fish water. When the potatoes are soft, add fish, milk, or cream. Heat but do not boil! Roll crackers and add to chowder. Season to taste and serve.

Rural Route 1, Mahone Bay, Nova Scotia

NORTHEAST

Au Petit Robinson THIS is probably one of the few places in the world where your dinner will be served up in a tree. Diners sit on platforms in large trees along the riverbank. In case of rain there is an indoor dining room. Meals served daily from noon until midnight. Open May 21 to September 15.

FROGS' LEGS SAUTE PROVENCALE

Pare legs and soak in cold running water until they are rosy white. Dip in mixture of eggs and milk before rolling in seasoned flour. Fry in very hot clarified butter or good oil. Cook fast enough so they turn golden as they cook. Dry on a clean towel and arrange on a hot plate, and sprinkle with chopped parsley and lemon juice. Brown 2 tablespoons of butter, then add a little chopped garlic, shaking pan to brown garlic on all sides. When lightly colored, pour over legs and serve.

NORTHEAST

Isle Bizard, Quebec

PAINTING BY JOHN DAVENPORT

Winkler's SINCE 1881 the Winkler family has run this rathskeller restaurant on the edge of the business district. Deviled crab is one of the most asked-for specialties. Open for lunch from 11:30 a.m. to 2:00 p.m., and dinner from 5:00 p.m. to 8:30 p.m., except Sunday.

DEVILED CRAB

2 cups crab meat
2 cups bread crumbs
1 cup milk
1 dash dry mustard
2 teaspoons salt
1 dash cayenne
¼ cup melted butter
Crab shells

Mix crab meat with crumbs which have been moistened with milk; season with mustard, salt, cayenne, and melted butter. Mix well. Fill crab shells with mixture and sprinkle bread crumbs lightly on top of filled shells and dot with butter. Brown quickly in hot oven (500°). Serve piping hot. This is a meal for 6.

1419 French Street, Wilmington, Delaware

SOUTHEAST

2

Iron Gate Inn A PICTURESQUE dining spot housed
in the former stables of General Nelson A. Miles, with a large
fireplace, copper and brass decorations, and hunt scenes. Six
blocks from the White House. Open for lunch and dinner.
Closed July 2 through 16 and December 21 through 28.

BREAST OF CHICKEN, BAKED IN CREAM

Cover a tender fowl to about two-thirds of its height in salted and peppered water. Stew slowly and carefully so that chicken retains its flavor. When tender, remove from broth and cool. Carefully remove the breast and place either in individual casseroles or in 1 large, shallow casserole. Cover with coffee cream and sprinkle heavily with paprika. Bake in moderate oven about 20 minutes or until the cream has thickened and looks a bit like custard. The breast of 1 chicken makes 3 to 4 servings.

1734 N Street, Northwest, Washington, D. C.

Kitty Knight House

THIS 1775 inn finds favor with nearly everybody but the snapping turtles in the nearby Sassafras River, who regularly find themselves popped into the stew. Breakfast, lunch, and dinner except Monday. Closed November 1 through March 31. Overnight accommodations.

SNAPPER STEW

Dress a 5- to 10-pound snapping turtle, saving only meat and eggs. Cook in water until tender; then remove from stock. For each pound of meat add to stock and cook slowly:

2 carrots, chopped
2 stalks celery, chopped
2 potatoes, diced

1 teaspoon minced onion
2 whole cloves
2 ounces dry sherry
Salt and pepper to taste

After cooking, add browned flour to thicken. Replace meat and eggs in stew. Serve piping hot. The stew should be thick enough to eat with a fork.

U.S. 213, Georgetown, Maryland

O'Donnell's Sea Grill

LOCATED on the site of historic Tiber Creek, this restaurant specializes in sea food, much of it being hauled in daily from Chesapeake Bay. Open for lunch and dinner from 11:00 a.m. to 3:00 a.m. Closed Christmas Day.

LOBSTER THERMIDOR

1- to 1½-pound lobster, cooked
Butter
1 jigger sherry
½ cup cream sauce
Pimento strips
Mushroom buttons
Parmesan cheese, grated

Split lobster back from center and remove solid meat. Sauté in butter; stir in sherry with cream sauce. Replace in lobster shell, garnish with strips of pimento and mushroom buttons. Sprinkle with grated cheese. Bake in moderate oven until brown. Makes a single serving.

1207-1221 E Street, Northwest, Washington, D. C.

Normandy Farm

OWNED and operated by Marjory Hendricks, this country restaurant is authentically French Provincial in decoration, with high-raftered beams in the dining room and huge stone fireplaces glistening with antique copper and brass. Open for lunch and dinner from 12:30 p.m. to 10:00 p.m. Reservations advisable.

POPOVERS

2 eggs
2 cups sifted flour
2 teaspoons salt
2 cups milk

Beat eggs until frothy; add flour sifted with salt and 1 cup of milk. Beat mixture well, then add remaining milk and beat again until smooth. Chill batter in the refrigerator. Grease iron muffin pan with unsalted vegetable fat and heat to sizzling point. Pour in batter and bake 15 minutes in a 450° oven and 20 minutes at 350°.

State Highway 189, Rockville, Maryland

SOUTHEAST

Park View Inn ONE of the oldest resorts in the country, this lovely inn facing the State Park at Berkeley Springs is adjacent to mineral springs and baths. It is open the year round. It is run on the American plan, but you can stop in for breakfast, lunch, or dinner. Reservations preferred.

CRAB CAKES

1 pound crab meat
2 heaping tablespoons mayonnaise
2 eggs, beaten lightly
½ teaspoon Worcestershire Sauce
½ teaspoon red pepper
¼ teaspoon salt
20 crackers

Combine all the ingredients in the order listed, except the crackers. Break (do not roll) the crackers very fine and add to crab-meat mixture. Mix well. Form into cakes and fry in fat till brown. Serve with tartar sauce.

Williamsburg Lodge

AT THIS pleasant, informal inn sea food is a specialty. Breakfast, lunch, and dinner are served; coffee shop open until 11:00 p.m. Overnight accommodations and recreation facilities.

WILLIAMSBURG CLAM CHOWDER

1 cup large chowder clams
1 cup cold water
3 ounces salt pork, diced
½ cup celery strips
1 medium-size onion
1 large-size potato
1 tablespoon green pepper
½ teaspoon thyme
1 cup tomatoes
Salt and pepper
½ tablespoon sherry
Parsley to taste

Put clams in boiler; cover with water. Simmer 15 minutes, remove from fire, and strain through cheese cloth. Pick and wash clams; put through a food chopper. Fry salt pork until crisp; add celery, onion, potatoes, and pepper, all chopped. Add clams and stock, thyme, tomatoes, salt, and pepper. Cook on a slow fire, stirring very often for an hour. Remove from fire, add sherry, and finish with chopped parsley. Makes 6 generous servings.

South England Street, Williamsburg, Virginia

SOUTHEAST

95

PAINTING BY DOUGLAS A. JONES

The Town House   A PEANUT pioneer's mansion has been lavishly restored to give this spot an authentic air of Southern elegance. If you're a real peanut lover, you'll want to visit the nearby Planters Nut and Chocolate Company factory. Breakfast, lunch, and dinner served. Overnight accommodations and vacation facilities.

DELUXE PEANUT PIE

1 cup parched peanuts
2 eggs, beaten
1 cup Karo Syrup (Blue Label)
⅛ teaspoon salt
1 teaspoon vanilla
1 cup sugar
2 tablespoons melted butter
   or margarine
1 pie shell, unbaked

Mix ingredients together, adding peanuts last. Pour into 9-inch pie pan lined with unbaked crust. Bake in hot oven, 400°, for 40 minutes or until filling fails to adhere to a silver knife inserted in the center of the pie. If you prefer, tarts may be made from this recipe. It will serve 6 to 8.

South High Street, Franklin, Virginia

2
SOUTHEAST
96

Skyline Terrace Restaurant THROUGH

the giant picture windows in the semicircular dining room, patrons here have a breathtaking view of mountains with every course. It's at the edge of Shenandoah National Park. Open for breakfast, lunch, and dinner from 7:00 a.m. to 8:30 p.m. Overnight accommodations.

GRILLED VIRGINIA HAM STEAK

Wash ham thoroughly in warm water to remove curing ingredients. Cover ham completely with cold water and allow to soak overnight. Remove and dry. Place in refrigerator to chill, then slice into steaks about ⅜ inch in thickness.

Place steaks in a lightly greased, very hot, old-fashioned iron skillet, over a medium flame. Turn frequently. Just before removing, pour into the skillet ½ cup water to which you have added ½ cup black coffee. Serve at once with this gravy.

Skyline Drive, Front Royal, Virginia

PAINTING BY DOUGLAS A. JONES

Half Way House

THIS historic restaurant acquired its name because it was just halfway on the stagecoach route between Petersburg and Richmond. It was built in 1760 on a grant of land from George II of England. Famous guests read like a page from your history book—Washington, Lafayette, and Patrick Henry are a few of them. Dinner served every day except Monday.

HALF WAY HOUSE GREEN BEANS

1 quart cooked green beans (snap or string)
3 to 4 strips bacon
2 tablespoons sugar
1 medium-sized onion, chopped fine
4 medium-sized tomatoes
Salt and pepper to taste

Fry bacon till very crisp; then remove from fat. Fry onion in bacon fat till light brown. Add tomatoes, sugar, salt, and pepper and simmer until tomatoes are soft. Add beans. Top mixture with crumbled bacon strips just before serving.

U. S. 1, Richmond, Virginia

2

SOUTHEAST

The Virginian Hotel APPOMATTOX, the Natural Bridge, and the homes of Lee and Jackson are in the vicinity of this modern hotel. Breakfast, lunch, and dinner served. Overnight accommodations and recreation facilities.

CUMBERLAND SAUCE

3 tablespoons red currant jelly
2 tablespoons strained
    orange juice
1 tablespoon strained
    lemon juice
1 teaspoon mustard
1 teaspoon coralline pepper
½ teaspoon ground ginger
    Peel of one orange

Stir jelly in saucepan over low flame until liquid. Cool, then add orange juice, lemon juice, mustard, pepper, and ginger. Peel orange so that white pulp is removed from skin; shred and cover with cold water and bring to a boil. Drain off water and add shredded orange peel to the mixture. This delicious sauce is served here with hot or cold slices of Virginia Smithfield ham.

Hotel Raleigh

THE Oyster Bar, now in the famous grill room of this hotel, was established in 1846 by the grandfather of the present owner. This was once a favorite stopping place for Edgar Allan Poe. Open for breakfast, lunch, and dinner. Overnight accommodations.

OLD VIRGINIA CORN CAKES

3 eggs
1 pint milk
1 pound water-ground corn meal, unbolted
½ teaspoon salt
1 teaspoon baking powder
1 cup melted lard

Beat eggs well and add milk. Sift meal and mix with salt, baking powder, and melted lard, and then mix with eggs and milk. Cook on a hot griddle greased with bacon rind. This recipe serves 6.

Ninth and Bank Streets, Richmond, Virginia

Beaumont Inn

THIS inn is housed in a spacious old Southern mansion furnished with antiques and set amidst a century-old forest. Once it was a college. Breakfast, lunch, and dinner daily. Closed December 1 to March 1. Reservations necessary for Sunday. Overnight accommodations.

ASPARAGUS SOUFFLE

1 cup asparagus, cut
1 level tablespoon flour
1 egg, beaten
1¼ cups milk
1 level tablespoon sugar
½ teaspoon salt
1 tablespoon butter, melted

Mix asparagus and flour; then combine with mixture of beaten egg and milk. Stir well. Add sugar, seasonings, and butter. Bake in moderate oven, stirring occasionally until mixture begins to thicken. Bake until firm but not long enough to bake dry.

PAINTING BY C. F. KORTEN

The Old House Restaurant   LOCATED

in an ante-bellum house, this restaurant specializes in French and Creole cookery. Chefs are delighted to give out their recipes. Lunch and dinner except Sunday and Christmas Day.

FLOUNDER ON PAPIER D'ARGENT

½-pound fillet of flounder
1 ounce white wine
1 ounce beef consommé
1 bay leaf
1 small celery leaf
1 egg yolk
Salt, pepper, chopped parsley

Mix white wine and beef consommé, add bay leaf and celery leaf, and poach flounder fillet briefly in this liquid. Spread 12-inch square of aluminum foil in bottom of another pan and place poached flounder on it. Thicken liquid in which flounder was poached with egg yolk, salt, pepper, and chopped parsley, and pour over flounder. Fold tinfoil about fillet, pinching ends together to form tight seal. Bake in hot oven for 10 minutes and serve fillet wrapped in tinfoil. This makes a single serving.

432 South Fifth Street, Louisville, Kentucky

Old Talbott Tavern THE love of things an-
tique "does not extend to bathtubs" at this 170-year-old inn.
You can sleep in the same room occupied by exiled Louis
Philippe in 1800 and still enjoy all modern conveniences.
Breakfast, lunch, and dinner. Overnight accommodations.

CHICKEN PAN PIE

Boil a 5- to 6-pound chicken until
well done. Cut up fowl and arrange
whole wings and smaller pieces with
bone in a baking pan. Thicken gravy
and pour over chicken in baking dish.
Season to taste with salt and pepper.
Cover with a thin crust, similar to pie
dough, and bake in moderate oven until crust is browned.

BUTTERMILK BISCUITS

½ cup lard
3 cups flour, sifted
½ level teaspoon salt
½ level teaspoon soda
3 level teaspoons baking powder
1¼ cups buttermilk

Cut lard into mixture of dry ingredients. Slowly add buttermilk. Roll onto
floured board and cut. Bake in 425°
oven 15 minutes.

Court House Square, Bardstown, Kentucky

SOUTHEAST 2

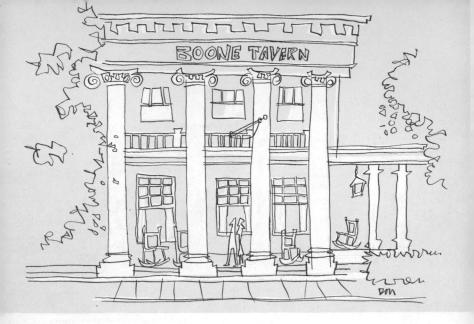

Boone Tavern   BEREA COLLEGE operates this inn, and 90 per cent of the staff are students earning their expenses. Some of the furniture is student-made; all the vegetables come from student gardens. Breakfast, lunch, and dinner. Overnight accommodations and recreation facilities.

KENTUCKY LEMON PIE

5 eggs
1½ cups Karo syrup (white)
1 cup sugar
Juice of 2 lemons
Rind of 1 lemon
¼ cup butter

This recipe, concocted by host Richard Hougen himself, is a specialty.

Beat eggs well; add syrup. Add sugar, lemon juice, and grated rind. Add butter and beat together until well mixed. Pour into unbaked pie shell and bake on the lower shelf of a moderate (375°) oven for 10 minutes; move to a middle shelf and reduce the heat to 350° for 30 to 40 minutes.

Berea College Campus, Berea, Kentucky

The Hut   A BEAUTIFUL outdoor terrace is open during the summer months for dining and dancing. Meals are from 6:30 a.m. to 10:00 p.m. daily. A. M. Lavinder is the owner.

TOSSED APPLE SALAD BOWL

2 raw apples, unpeeled
2 oranges
¼ cup peanuts, chopped
2 teaspoons onion, minced
2 cups raw green cabbage, finely shredded
¼ cup French dressing

Cut apples into small wedges and divide orange into sections. Place in salad bowl with peanuts, onion, and cabbage. Add dressing before serving and toss well. Serves 4.

APPLE CRISP

4 cups apples, sliced
¼ cup water
¾ cup sugar
½ cup pastry or cake flour
1 teaspoon cinnamon
¼ teaspoon salt
6 tablespoons butter

Arrange apples in baking dish. Add water. Combine dry ingredients; blend in butter till mixture is crumbly. Pour over apples. Bake uncovered about an hour at 350°. Serves 6.

Off U.S. 220 (2 mi. n. of Martinsville), Roanoke, Va.   **SOUTHEAST**

PAINTING BY CHARLES HARPER

Oelsner's Colonial Tavern HOME-COOKED

meals served in a friendly, homey atmosphere distinguish this attractive restaurant and make it a favorite stop for motorists. Lunch and dinner served every day.

PINEAPPLE CREAM PIE

1 cup cubed pineapple
3 tablespoons flour
1 cup sugar
2 egg yolks
2 cups milk
1 tablespoon butter
1 pie shell, baked

Meringue
Combine flour and sugar before mixing with egg yolks and milk. Cook until thick, then add butter and pineapple. Pour into pie shell and cover with meringue. Brown meringue in oven and serve.

U.S. 25 and 42, Covington, Kentucky

Norris Park Tea Room

IN the recreation area surrounding TVA's Norris Dam, this inn commands a delightful view. Breakfast, lunch, and dinner; overnight and vacation facilities. Open May 1 to September 15.

NORRIS PARK ROLLS

½ cup shortening
¼ cup sugar
1 cake yeast
1 egg, beaten
4½ cups flour
1 teaspoon salt
½ teaspoon baking powder
   (double action)
¼ teaspoon soda

Cream shortening and sugar, add ½ cup boiling water, and let stand until lukewarm. Dissolve yeast in ½ cup cool water and combine with creamed mixture and beaten egg. Sift flour, salt, baking powder, and soda together, and add to first mixture. Let rise to double bulk in greased bowl. Place in refrigerator; shape dough into rolls in greased pan, brush tops with butter, and let rise to double bulk in warm place. Bake.

Norris Dam, Norris, Tennessee

New Gatlinburg Inn

THERE's a breathtaking view of Mt. Le Conte here. Breakfast, lunch, and dinner. Overnight accommodations and vacation facilities.

COCONUT PIE

    1½ cups fresh shredded coconut
    1 tablespoon granulated gelatin
    4 eggs, separated
    1 cup sugar
    Pinch of salt
    ½ cup cream
    ½ cup cream, whipped
    1 teaspoon vanilla or sherry
    flavoring

Soak gelatin in ½ cup cold water 5 minutes. Beat egg yolks, adding ½ cup sugar, salt, and ½ cup cream. Cook in double boiler until thick and add the soaked gelatin. Beat whites stiff, gradually adding the ½ cup sugar. When the custard mixture has cooled, fold in the whites, coconut, and flavoring. Pour in pie shell and chill thoroughly in refrigerator. Just before serving, spread ½ cup cream that has been whipped and sweetened over top of pie and sprinkle with remaining coconut.

PIE CRUST

Crush 20 chocolate cookies until very fine and add ¼ cup melted margarine. Pat into 9-inch pie pan and chill in refrigerator.

U.S. 441, Gatlinburg, Tennessee

SOUTHEAST

Cupboard Tea Room

OWNER Mrs. Carl Hickerson says the nut soufflé is a prized recipe. Other specialties are homemade rolls, chess pie, and candied yams. Lunch served daily, dinner every day except Sunday, when lunch only is served.

NUT SOUFFLE

8 egg whites
2 cups sugar
1 cup chopped pecans
4 cooked prunes, chopped
Pinch of salt
1 teaspoon vanilla

Beat egg whites till very stiff; then beat in other ingredients in the order listed. Pour the mixture into a pan 10 inches long, 2 inches deep, and 5 inches wide, lightly greased with butter. Bake in a slow oven (300° to 320°) for 45 to 60 minutes on the middle rack. Place a pan of water under the soufflé to prevent burning. When soufflé is cold, serve it with scoops of whipped cream.

Buckhorn Inn THIS hostelry is located on a hill dramatically facing the main range of the Great Smokies. You're an easy car's ride from many beauty spots here. Breakfast, lunch, and dinner served. Overnight accommodations and vacation facilities. Reservations necessary. Closed from November 1 to April 1.

CORN PUDDING

2½ cups cream-style corn
3 eggs, beaten slightly
1 cup milk
1 teaspoon salt
¼ teaspoon pepper
1 tablespoon minced onion
1 pimento, chopped

½ green pepper, chopped
2 tablespoons butter

Mix ingredients together and bake in a 325° oven for an hour. This makes an interesting and colorful way to serve part of the vegetable course for either holiday meals or party fare.

2

SOUTHEAST *State Highway 73, 5 miles east of Gatlinburg, Tennessee*
110

PAINTING BY CHARLES HARPER

Frederick Hotel

GOOD food and a friendly welcome await the traveler who stops at this hotel's fine dining spot, called the Bonanza Room. Breakfast, lunch, and dinner served daily. Overnight accommodations.

DUTCH FAMILIE CAKE

- ½ cup shortening
- 2 squares bitter chocolate
- 1 cup sugar
- 2 eggs, well beaten
- 1 cup apple sauce
- 1 teaspoon vanilla
- ½ cup pecans, chopped
- 1 cup flour
- ½ teaspoon baking powder
- ¼ teaspoon baking soda
- ¼ teaspoon salt

Melt and blend shortening and chocolate. Cool; then stir in sugar, eggs, apple sauce, vanilla, and pecans. Sift flour, baking powder, soda, and salt together; then stir into chocolate mixture. Pour into 8-inch square pan and bake for 35 to 40 minutes in 350° oven. Cut into portion squares. Serves 8 to 10. Mr. Leo Ree, the hotel's catering manager, brought this recipe from his home in Haarlem, Holland.

Fourth Avenue and Tenth Street, Huntington, W. Va.

Holly Inn

HERE, in "America's golfing paradise," breakfast, lunch, and dinner are served. Overnight accommodations and recreation facilities. Open October 1 to May 15. Reservations necessary middle of March through April.

CHOW MEIN

Meat of one large boiled fowl, cut julienne
1 stalk celery
1 pound white onions
½ pound fresh mushrooms
¼ pound ground meat
1 pint water chestnuts
1 pint bamboo hearts
1½ cups stock from the fowl
½ quart bean sprouts
Soy sauce

Slice celery, onions, and mushrooms in a pot with a small amount of stock. Cover tightly and allow to simmer slowly so they will make their own liquor. When these are half cooked, add ground beef and stock of fowl. Boil slowly for 1 hour. Add chestnuts, bamboo hearts, dark meat of fowl, and bean sprouts. Bring to a boil, season, add soy sauce to taste, and serve with fried noodles and boiled rice. Garnish with white meat of the fowl. Serves 8.

SOUTHEAST

Pinehurst, North Carolina

General Lewis Hotel THIS is a new hotel built in an early American style, on the site where General Andrew Lewis blazed the giant oak and where the Battle of Lewisburg was fought in 1863. Breakfast, lunch, and dinner served. Overnight accommodations.

CANDIED SWEET POTATOES WITH PEANUTS

6 medium-size sweet potatoes
½ cup brown sugar
1 cup boiling water
4 tablespoons butter
½ teaspoon salt
2 teaspoons chopped peanuts

Pare and slice sweet potatoes. Make a syrup of sugar, water, butter, and salt. Put in a shallow baking dish with potatoes. Bake in slow oven for 1 hour or until candied. When nearly done, sprinkle with chopped peanuts and brown lightly.

Nu-Wray Inn

FOR three generations the Wray family have run this friendly mountain inn. You'll want to try their real Southern food and especially their country ham, cured in their own smokehouse. All meals served, except Sunday supper. Overnight accommodations and vacation facilities.

HOLIDAY SALAD

1 cup sugar
1 cup raw cranberries, ground
1 package lemon gelatin
½ cup boiling water
1 cup orange juice
2 teaspoons grated orange rind
9-ounce can crushed pineapple
½ cup pecan meats, broken
1 cup chopped celery

Mix sugar and berries together, and let stand several hours. Add gelatin to boiling water, stirring until dissolved. Stir in orange juice and other ingredients. Pour into mold and set in refrigerator. Serve on crisp lettuce garnished with mayonnaise.

U. S. 19E, Burnsville, North Carolina

Tapoco Lodge

HIGH in the Great Smoky Mountains, this inn is picturesquely situated on the west bank of the Cheoah River. Breakfast, lunch, and dinner served. Overnight accommodations. Reservations advised.

MAC'S PANCAKES

4 eggs
1 cup sugar
4 tablespoons baking powder
1½ teaspoons salt
3 cups milk
5 cups flour, approx.
1½ cups melted shortening

Mix eggs, sugar, baking powder, and salt, and add milk. Whip ingredients and add flour to get desired consistency. Blend shortening in. Recipe makes about 32 average-size pancakes. Serve with maple syrup, mountain honey, or powdered sugar and jam. Makes a Sunday night supper.

The Gold Eagle ORIGINALLY this was the planta-
tion home of Henry DeSaussure, designer of the first gold
dollar (or gold eagle) and first director of the U. S. Mint by
the appointment of President Washington. Breakfast served
year round; dinner from November 1 to May 1. Overnight and
vacation facilities. Reservations requested.

BANANA MEAT ROLLS

> 2 bananas, sliced
> 1 cup ground cold meat
> 1½ small onions, chopped
> 1 celery heart, chopped
> Butter
> Biscuit dough
> Cream sauce
> Chopped parsley

Sauté the onion and celery in butter
and combine with cold meat and sliced
bananas. Roll biscuit dough thin and
spread the mixture over it. Roll dough
jelly-roll fashion and slice pieces off
the completed roll. Bake in a greased
pan until browned. Serve with cream
sauce and chopped parsley.

2

SOUTHEAST

116

Bay and New Streets, Beaufort, South Carolina

PAINTING BY WILLIAM HALSEY

Brewton Inn and Tea Room THE brick
tea room and guest houses here date back to 1735, when they
were the coach houses of the General Miles Brewton estate.
Lunch and dinner served every day except Sunday; breakfast
to house guests only. Overnight accommodations and recreation
facilities. Open from October 15 to middle or end of May.

SHRIMP CREOLE

3 cups freshly cooked shrimp
2 medium-size onions
1 green pepper
1½ cups celery
4 tablespoons bacon drippings
1-quart can tomatoes
3 tablespoons tomato paste
Salt and pepper to taste

Cut up onions, green pepper, and celery. Fry in bacon drippings for 15 or 20 minutes. Add the tomatoes and tomato paste. Let simmer slowly to a thick consistency for 30 to 45 minutes. Add pepper sauce to taste. 15 minutes before serving, add shrimp. Serve with dry rice.

75 Church Street, Charleston, South Carolina

The Poinsett Hotel

BECAUSE of its old-fashioned Southern hospitality and cuisine, this modern hotel has an aura of bygone days. Its famous spoon bread is served to everyone at lunch and dinner by a costumed "mammy." Breakfast, lunch, and dinner are served. Overnight accommodations.

SPOON BREAD

1 cup white corn meal
1½ cups boiling water
1 egg
1 tablespoon butter
1 cup buttermilk
1 teaspoon baking soda
¾ teaspoon salt
½ cup milk or light cream, sour or sweet

Pour boiling water over corn meal; beat well, then let cool slightly. Mix in remaining ingredients (except ½ cup milk or cream). Pour batter into hot, greased 7-inch baking dish. Bake in 350° oven for 30 to 40 minutes. If soft top is desired, add a few spoonfuls milk or cream from time to time while bread is baking, and bake 1 hour altogether.

SOUTHEAST
118

South Main Street, Greenville, South Carolina

Sunset Farm

A MILE from the entrance to Great Smoky Mountain National Park, this establishment is open for breakfast, lunch, and dinner. Overnight accommodations. Closed April 15 to October 31.

CHOCOLATE RUM PIE

2 cups milk, scalded
4 eggs, separated
½ cup sugar
1¼ tablespoons cornstarch
1½ squares chocolate
1 teaspoon vanilla
1 cooked pie crust
1 tablespoon gelatin
3 tablespoons rum
¼ teaspoon cream of tartar
1 cup whipped cream
Chocolate slivers

Combine milk, egg yolks, sugar, and cornstarch. Cook 20 minutes, stirring, till mixture forms thin custard. To 1 cup of this, add chocolate squares and vanilla; pour mixture into crust. To remaining custard, add gelatin and 4 tablespoons water. Let mixture cool but not get too thick. Beat egg whites into meringue; add rum and tartar. When custard in crust sets, add this mixture. Chill till firm. Top with whipped cream and chocolate slivers.

U.S. 19, Whittier, North Carolina

PAINTING BY J. C. LEAVELL

Blue Moon Inn FOR over 30 years Leila Dowe has run this quaint restaurant. Lunch and dinner, except Sunday and Monday. Closed in August. Reservations necessary.

CHICKEN COUNTRY CAPTAIN

3 fryers cut in pieces
1 teaspoon salt
½ teaspoon pepper
Paprika
2 cloves garlic, chopped
4 medium onions, chopped
3 green peppers, chopped fine
3 No. 2 cans tomatoes
1 dash cayenne
½ teaspoon thyme
1 teaspoon curry powder
½ cup chopped parsley
1 cup currants
½ pound blanched toasted almonds

Roll chickens in mixture of flour, salt, pepper and paprika. Fry in deep fat until golden brown. Place in a roaster, add ½ cup hot water, and steam slowly. To fat add garlic, onions, and green peppers, and brown slightly. Add ½ cup water and cook 10 to 15 minutes. Blend in tomatoes and remaining seasonings. Cook until smooth. Pour over chicken and cook until tender, about 1 hour. Add currants and almonds and serve with wild rice.

SOUTHEAST

120

1816 Goode Street, Montgomery, Alabama

Purefoy Hotel

"ALL YOU CAN EAT" is the boast of Manager Ed Hyde as he describes this hotel's bountiful family-style meals. Breakfast and dinner are served throughout the week except on Sundays. Overnight accommodations and recreation facilities are available.

RAW CRANBERRY SAUCE

  1 quart cranberries
  2 Delicious apples
  ½ orange peel
  2 large oranges
  2 cups sugar

Put cranberries, apples, and orange peel through food chopper. Cut oranges in small sections with scissors and add sugar. Stir mixture well and set in refrigerator. It will keep for several days. At the Purefoy it is served as a sauce; or congealed as a salad with 2 cups of pecans added; or as a dessert in little parfait glasses. Halve this recipe for a small family.

½ block west of U.S. 231, Talladega, Alabama

Châlet Suzanne

THIS beautiful year-round vacation spot is set amidst 230 acres of orange groves at Lake Suzanne. Meals are served on a terrace overlooking the lake or in a tree-shaded patio. Breakfast, lunch, dinner, 7:00 a.m. to 9:00 p.m. Reservations preferred.

ORANGE BREAD

1 egg
1 cup milk
1 tablespoon fat
2½ cups flour
1 teaspoon salt
3 rounding tablespoons sugar
4 teaspoons baking powder
1 heaping cup candied
  Orange peel, grated

Beat the egg thoroughly and add to milk. Cut fat into the flour. Add salt, sugar, and baking powder. Stir in milk-and-egg mixture slowly. Add orange peel, put into a greased loaf pan, and bake in a medium oven. This delicious bread will go with fruit and gelatin salads, add variety to the bread tray at dinner, or make a party sandwich with a filling of cream cheese.

SOUTHEAST

U.S. 27, 4 miles north of Lake Wales, Florida

The Garden OWNER Rudy Chmelik received his food training when he was an apprentice to the Austrian Court. Today his restaurant is one of the most popular in the South. Lunch and dinner from noon till 1:00 a.m., May to December. Reservations necessary.

BANANA FRITTERS

8 bananas, sliced
1 cup flour
1 teaspoon baking powder
1 teaspoon sugar
Pinch of salt
1 egg
½ cup milk

Mix a batter with the flour, baking powder, sugar, salt, egg, and milk. Beat well and dip thick slices of banana into the batter. Drop a teaspoon of banana and batter into deep fat and fry until golden brown and fluffy. This recipe will make 8 hearty servings. The fritters are served with a series of other Southern vegetables at The Garden. Try them as something different in a fruit or vegetable course!

2235 Southwest Eighth Street, Miami, Florida

The Georgian Tea Room

SINCE 1929 this tea room has been located in an interesting old pink house, a former home of one of the city's earliest settlers. Open for lunch, tea, and dinner, except Sundays and national holidays.

CAROLINA TRIFLE

1 pint whipped cream
1 quart boiled custard
 Almond extract, brandy, or sherry
1 lemon-flavored sponge cake

Flavor the cream and custard with either almond extract, brandy, or sherry. Slice the sponge cake very thin and place a slice of the cake on a dish and cover it first with a layer of custard, then a thin layer of whipped cream. Repeat the process, using all of the cake slices, and top it off with a layer of whipped cream. Chill and serve.

23 Abercorn Street, Savannah, Georgia

Wedgwood Inn

THE largest collection of old Wedgwood in the South is found here. Hal Douglas is the manager of this establishment's three fine dining rooms. Lunch and dinner served daily from 11:30 a.m. to 9:00 p.m.

CHRISTMAS PUDDING

1 cup bread crumbs
1½ cups hot milk
10 egg whites
6 ounces cake flour
1½ teaspoons baking soda
2 teaspoons nutmeg
2 teaspoons cinnamon
1 teaspoon mace
1 pound raisins
1 pound currants
1 pound chopped citrus fruits
½ cup fruit juice, any kind
1 cup currant or guava jelly

Soak bread crumbs in hot milk 10 minutes. Beat egg whites till stiff. Combine remaining ingredients; add crumb-and-milk mixture; then fold in egg whites. Pour batter into greased molds and steam for 3½ hours. Recipe makes three 2-pound puddings. The chef here serves pudding with rum hard sauce.

Fourth St. and Eighteenth Ave., S., St. Petersburg, Fla.

SOUTHEAST

2

The Lighthouse

ONE of the most valuable things owner S. D. Macris brought with him from the Isle of Cephalonia, Greece, some 30 years ago, was a collection of unusual recipes. The restaurant is just a stone's throw from the ocean. Lunch and dinner from noon to midnight.

RED SNAPPER A LA LIGHTHOUSE

3 pounds red snapper fillets
Salt and pepper to taste
3 jiggers olive oil
Juice of 1 lemon
1 teaspoon oregano
3 cloves garlic

Sprinkle the fillets with salt and pepper and place in a broiler. Mix oil, lemon juice, and oregano together and pour over fish. Broil 40 minutes (or until tender) in a 350° oven. While fish is broiling, cut garlic into small pieces and fry in olive oil. Pour garlic over fish before serving. Just add some crispy shoestring potatoes and buttered asparagus to the plates, and dinner is served.

Baker's Haulover, Route A1A, Miami Beach, Florida

Columbia Restaurant

SINCE 1905, the Hernandez family has run this top-rate eating place. You can choose to enjoy your meal on their patio, equipped with a sliding glass roof, or in air-conditioned dining rooms. Open 8:30 a.m. to 1:30 a.m. Reservations advisable during winter.

STEAK CAPUCHINA

1 steak
2 teaspoons butter
1 small onion, chopped
½ cup chicken livers, chopped
Salt and pepper to taste
½ cup mushrooms
3 ounces dark red wine

Put butter into sauce pan and fry onions in it. When they're almost done, add the chicken livers, salt, and pepper. When they're browned, add mushrooms and wine. Then grill your steak. Take plain wrapping paper and wrap it around the steak. Cover bottom of roasting pan with the sauce and cover the paper-wrapped steak with it. Then bake in a slow oven (275-300°F.) for 10 minutes.

Loffler Brothers' Oyster House OWNERS

Lenny and Andy Loffler, ex-GI's, are the third generation of dietetic experts in their family. Their restaurant is highly favored by a fish-hungry populace. Open for lunch and dinner from 11:30 a.m. to 9:00 p.m.

SEA FOOD A LA LOFFLER

    1 pound fillet of fish
    4 lobster tails
    ½ pint scallops
    ½ pint shrimp

Cut fish in strips 1½ inches wide. Split lobster tails. Steam scallops, shrimp, lobster tails (with shell), and fish until tender. Shell and de-vein shrimp. Remove meat from lobster tails. Divide into four portions and place in individual casseroles. Pour sauce (see below) over them and broil in oven under medium heat until golden brown. Serve immediately.

SAUCE

Melt ¼ pound butter in pan and add ⅓ cup flour. Slowly stir in 2½ cups milk and season with salt, pepper, ¼ pound grated cheese, and 1 teaspoon sherry. This sauce also blends well with other dishes.

280 Alhambra Circle, Coral Gables, Florida

Gary's Duck Inn

"THE secret of our tender shrimp is to fry them raw," says owner C. Gary Starling. People from miles around swarm to this restaurant to sample his unusual shrimp dishes. Open for lunch and dinner.

JUMBO SHRIMP

2 pounds raw shrimp—jumbo size
1¼ pounds cracker meal
1 egg
1 cup milk
  Deep fat

SAUCE

4 cups catsup
4 tablespoons horseradish
3 tablespoons mayonnaise

Peel and clean raw shrimp and roll in cracker meal. Dip in batter of egg and milk, and roll again in cracker meal. When rolling shrimp, curve them so that the ends make handy holders. Fry in deep fat for 3 minutes. Mix sauce ingredients together and serve with French fries and hot corn sticks.

3974 S. Orange Blossom Trail, Orlando, Florida

Dolphin Tavern

WHILE giant porpoises eat dinner at the Marine Studios next door, you may have yours here. Open lunch and dinner, 11:30 a.m. to 8:00 p.m. Smorgasbord 11:30 a.m. to 3:00 p.m. Overnight accommodations.

CLAM CHOWDER A LA LOUIS THOMAS

2 quarts clams, finely chopped by hand, and clam juice
¾ pound salt pork
8 good-sized onions, chopped
2 green peppers, chopped
2 Datyl peppers, chopped
3 cloves garlic, chopped
2 #2½ cans tomatoes
Juice of 1 lemon, with grated peel
6 bay leaves, fresh or dried
3 tablespoons Lea & Perrins sauce
1 teaspoon Tabasco sauce
1 cup Heinz catsup or chili sauce
3 tablespoons sugar
4 medium-sized potatoes, diced

Dice salt pork and sauté over low fire. Add onions, peppers, and garlic. Cook until delicately browned. Add tomatoes, lemon juice, grated peel, sugar, and seasonings; bring to a slow boil. Add potatoes and cook until tender. Add chopped clams and juice. Simmer at least 20 minutes and serve.

SOUTHEAST

State Highway A1A, Marineland, Florida

Nashville House　IF YOU'RE partial to a real home-cooked meal of country delicacies in the foothills of the Cumberlands, you'll find this spot to your liking. Under the same roof is an old-time rural store where you can buy many old favorites that have been banished from the shelves of the modern market. Lunch and dinner served, except Tuesday.

CREAM OF TURNIP SOUP

1 quart milk
1 onion
1 tablespoon flour
2 tablespoons butter, melted
2 cups grated raw turnip
1 teaspoon salt
　Parsley, chopped

Heat milk in double boiler with the onion, halved. Add flour and butter well blended, then the turnip and salt. Cook until the turnip is tender—about 10 minutes—then remove onion. Sprinkle chopped parsley over the soup just before serving. A giant bowl makes a hearty winter lunch.

Main and Van Buren Streets, Nashville, Indiana　　**NORTH CENTRAL**

Kopper Kettle   FOR nearly 100 years this restaurant has been a popular stopping place for hungry travelers. In the early days it was the stagecoach that pulled up at the friendly entranceway where today cars crowd. Open for lunch and dinner from 11:00 a.m. to 9:00 p.m. daily. Closed from December 1 to April 1.

SWEET-SOUR CUCUMBERS

1 dozen medium-size cucumbers
2 tablespoons salt
1 medium-size onion
2 cups sugar
½ teaspoon pepper
1 pint sweet whipping cream
1 pint vinegar

Wash, peel, and slice cucumbers and place in earthen jar. Add salt and sliced onion, then cover jar with cheesecloth, plate, and weight. Let stand 6 hours and drain off water. Add sugar and mix until dissolved; then add pepper and vinegar. Stir in cream. Put in refrigerator till cold and crisp.

3 NORTH CENTRAL

U.S. 52, Morristown, Indiana

Hawthorne Room

EXTRAORDINARILY good food and convenient location have made this a most popular dining spot. Try the fried chicken and homemade pastries. Meals from 11:00 a.m. to 9:00 p.m. Closed Christmas Day.

SOUR CREAM RAISIN PIE

1 cup brown sugar
2 tablespoons flour
½ teaspoon nutmeg
½ teaspoon cinnamon
¼ teaspoon salt
1 cup sour cream
3 egg yolks
1 cup raisins
3 egg whites
6 tablespoons sugar
1 baked pie shell

Combine brown sugar, flour, spices, salt, and sour cream in top of a double boiler and cook until thick. Beat egg yolks in separate dish and blend a little of the hot paste with them before stirring into mixture in double boiler. Cook for 5 minutes and add raisins. Cool. Place in baked pie shell and cover with meringue made with egg whites and sugar. Brown in oven.

North Meridian at 16th Street, Indianapolis, Indiana **NORTH CENTRAL** **3**

Red Brick Tavern NUMBERLESS travelers have been served at this friendly restaurant, halfway between Columbus and Springfield, since it opened its doors in 1837. Lunch and dinner served every day except Monday.

RED BRICK BANANA CREAM PIE

⅔ cup sugar
3½ tablespoons cornstarch
½ teaspoon salt
2½ cups milk
3 egg yolks, slightly beaten
1 teaspoon vanilla
1 pie shell, baked
2 bananas, sliced
Meringue

Combine the sugar, cornstarch, and salt in the top of a double boiler, stirring in the cold milk. Cook over boiling water until it thickens, stirring constantly. Cover and cook 15 minutes longer. Stir a little of the hot mixture into the slightly beaten egg yolks, then add the eggs to the hot pudding, and cook together for about 2 minutes, stirring constantly. Cool and add vanilla. Arrange sliced bananas in a baked pastry shell and pour in the cooled cream filling. Top with meringue and oven-brown it.

U.S. 40, Lafayette, Ohio

Restaurant Continentale

Restaurant Continentale THIS elegant salon is one of five excellent dining rooms at the Netherland Plaza Hotel. Lunch 11:30 a.m. to 2:00 p.m. every day except Sunday.

HUNGARIAN BEEF GOULASH

3 pounds beef, chuck or round
½ pound onions, diced
   Salt and pepper
½ pound fresh tomatoes
2 ounces "rosen" paprika
1 small clove garlic
1 pinch chopped caraway seeds
   Bouquet of vegetables
1½ pints water
¾ cup sour cream

Brown onions in saucepan with lard. Add beef cut in squares; season with salt and pepper. Cover pan and simmer 25 minutes in a moderate oven. Then stir in tomatoes, paprika, garlic, caraway seed, bouquet of vegetables, and water. Continue cooking 1½ hours. Remove meat, strain sauce, then mix meat and sauce together again. Add sour cream and serve. Makes 6 good portions.

Fifth and Race Streets, Cincinnati, Ohio

PAINTING BY CHARLES HARPER

The Spanish Inn AMUSING murals sketched by well-known artist patrons, unusual hand-carved furniture, and gleaming copper utensils hanging in the kitchen combine in this restaurant to suggest the Old World atmosphere of a Madrid café. Lunch and dinner every day except Sunday.

SOPA DE GARBANZOS (Chick-pea Soup)

1 pound garbanzos (chick-peas)
2½ quarts water
1 tablespoon paprika
3 tablespoons ham drippings
2 cloves garlic
1 cup rice
Salt to taste

Soak garbanzos overnight. Cook slowly for 2 hours in the water, adding more water when necessary to maintain the same amount of liquid. Fry the paprika in the ham drippings; add a little cold water to separate the fat from the sediment. Skim off the fat and add it to the soup with the garlic cloves, which have been lightly browned. Add the rice 15 minutes before garbanzos are done. Salt to taste.

3

NORTH CENTRAL

136

15 East Eighth Street, Cincinnati, Ohio

Gourmet Restaurant

A CRYSTAL ball in the sky, this restaurant atop the new Terrace Plaza Hotel seats only 56 diners. Guests are treated to a superb French cuisine, with a breathtaking view of the surrounding hills thrown in. Lunch and dinner, every day except Sunday. Reservations advisable.

CHRISTMAS PUDDING

½ pound citron, sliced thin
¼ pound lemon peel, sliced thin
¼ pound orange peel, sliced thin
2 pounds raisins, cut
2 pounds seedless raisins
2 pounds currants
1 pound beef suet, chopped fine
1 teaspoon salt
2 loaves white bread, crumbed
4 pounds sugar
4 quarts chopped apples
¼ pound blanched almonds, chopped coarsely
1 dozen eggs, well beaten
1 wineglass brandy

Mix together ingredients in the order given. Pack into buttered pudding bowls and cover with white cloth tied firmly in place. Place bowls in a basin filled with hot water and steam for 3 hours.

Sixth Street between Vine & Race, Cincinnati, Ohio   **NORTH CENTRAL**   3

PAINTING BY CHARLES HARPER

Valerio's Italian Restaurant

HERE the Valerio family, supervised by Mama Valerio, carry on a tradition of serving good foods. Garlic bread is a side treat with most meals. Lunch and dinner until midnight every day except Tuesday. Closed last two weeks of August, including Labor Day. Reservations necessary.

SCALLOPINI AL MARSALA

16 slices veal cutlet, ⅜ inch thick and 2 inches in diameter
1 teaspoon salt
½ teaspoon pepper
½ cup flour
5 tablespoons butter
¾ cup Marsala wine
4 sprigs parsley

Ask butcher to pound pieces of meat with heaviest cleaver to make them thin. Salt and pepper, dip in flour, and sauté in butter until brown on both sides. Pour wine over scallopini and sauté over low flame until wine gravy has slightly thickened. Serve with finely chopped parsley.

NORTH CENTRAL *114 East Sixth Street (second floor), Cincinnati, Ohio*

PAINTING BY ALEXANDER BALUCH

Hotel Phoenix Coffee Shop THE specialties of this popular dining room are homemade pies, breads, and crisp garden salads served with tangy dressings. Open from 6:00 a.m. to 9:00 p.m. Overnight accommodations.

FRENCH DRESSING

2 medium onions, chopped fine
½ cup sugar
1 teaspoon salt
1 tablespoon dry mustard
1 teaspoon white pepper
1 tablespoon paprika
1 #1 can tomato soup
1 cup corn oil

¾ cup vinegar
1 teaspoon horseradish

Marinate onions with sugar. Blend dry ingredients and add soup, corn oil, vinegar, and marinated onions. Beat well and blend in horseradish. Let stand an hour. This makes ¾ quart. Keep in refrigerator and serve chilled with your favorite salads.

305 South Main Street, Findlay, Ohio

NORTH CENTRAL 3
139

The Tivoli THIS restaurant is named for a famous resort in Denmark, the birthplace of the owners, Arne and Ernestine Nissen. They feature smorgasbord and authentic Scandinavian dishes. Open for lunch and dinner from 11:30 a.m. until 2:30 a.m. Closed Mondays and Christmas Day.

RUMBUDDING WITH SAUCE

3 egg yolks
6 tablespoons sugar
2 tablespoons rum
¼ teaspoon salt
1 tablespoon gelatin, unflavored
¾ cup cold water
1 cup whipping cream

Beat eggs and sugar well; add rum and salt. Soak gelatin in the water, dissolve over hot water, and add to egg mixture. As it thickens, stir in whipped cream. Chill in molds.

FRUIT SAUCE

Bring 1 cup fruit cocktail juice to a boil. Mix a little water with 1½ teaspoons cornstarch and pour into boiling juice; stir constantly. Add juice of ¼ lemon, a dash of rum, and red coloring. Chill and serve with pudding.

NORTH CENTRAL

4535 Monroe Street, Toledo, Ohio

3

Sid's Restaurant GUESTS here have a ringside seat on one of the world's busiest inland waterways, the St. Clair River. Against this backdrop, fish dishes are a must. Open weekdays 10:00 a.m. to 2:00 a.m.; Sundays, noon to 1:30 a.m., the year round.

DEEP-FRIED PICKEREL

Fillet the fish, rinse in cold water, and allow it to drain. Mix together 1 well-beaten egg and 2 measuring cups (1 pint) milk. Dip the pickerel in the batter and dust it with cracker crumbs. Sprinkle with paprika and fry in deep fat heated to 300°. When it's done it will have turned a golden brown and will bob to the top of the boiling fat. Serve with Sid's Tartar Sauce.

SID'S TARTAR SAUCE

⅓ portion chopped sweet pickles
⅔ portion mayonnaise
Small portion of lemon juice
Ground dry onion to taste
Dash of horseradish
Celery salt
Combine ingredients and chill.

9715 St. Clair River Drive, Algonac, Michigan

NORTH CENTRAL 3

Holiday House THIS restaurant, patterned after an English country inn, is set amidst extensive orchards. In fact, all of the fruits for its pies and pastries come from these trees. Meals are served from 12:00 to 8:00 p.m. every day except Monday. Smorgasbord every Thursday. Open May 1 to November 1.

VIENNESE APPLE STRUDEL

- 10 apples, peeled
- 2 cups bread crumbs
- ⅝ cup sugar
- Basic strudel dough
- ½ cup raisins
- ¼ teaspoon cinnamon
- 2 ounces chopped nuts (walnuts or almonds)
- ½ cup butter

Slice apples very thin. Fry crumbs golden brown in butter and add sugar. On basic strudel dough spread first apples, then crumbs, raisins, cinnamon, and nuts; then sprinkle with a little extra sugar and melted butter. Roll the strudel and place on oiled baking sheet. Dot with butter and bake in moderate oven until golden brown—about 45 to 60 minutes.

NORTH CENTRAL

U.S. 12, 3 miles south of St. Joseph, Michigan

Fox and Hounds Inn

AT this authentic replica of an English inn, the menu offers such British favorites as roast beef with Yorkshire pudding. Lunch, dinner, except Christmas and New Year's Day. Reservations advisable.

BEEFSTEAK AND KIDNEY PIE

1 pound veal kidney, diced
1 pound round steak, diced
½ pound fresh mushrooms
2 jiggers Burgundy wine
½ teaspoon salt
1 bay leaf
1 teaspoon Worcestershire sauce
3 tablespoons flour
1 pie crust, uncooked

Parboil the veal kidney in salt water for about 15 minutes; then wash it off in cold water. Parboil the round steak in salt water for 15 minutes and wash it off in cold water. Sauté steak till brown; add mushrooms and wine. Sauté mixture for 5 minutes. Add about 3 cups water to the round steak and add kidneys. Simmer for about an hour, with salt, bay leaf, and Worcestershire sauce added for flavor. Make a paste of flour and ½ cup water to thicken the gravy. Put filling into a casserole, cover with a flaky pie crust, and bake for ½ hour.

U.S. 10, Bloomfield Hills, Michigan

Dearborn Inn THIS Ford-built inn is within walking distance of such tourist attractions as Greenfield Village and the Henry Ford Museum. Breakfast, lunch, and dinner served. Overnight accommodations and recreation facilities.

PINEAPPLE WHIPPED CREAM PIE

1 #2½ can crushed pineapple
1 cup sugar
  Pinch of salt
  Juice of ½ lemon
2 tablespoons cornstarch
1 unbaked pie shell
  Whipped cream

Cook pineapple with sugar, salt, and lemon juice. Thicken with cornstarch. Pour into unbaked shell and bake for 30 minutes. Let cool; then serve topped with whipped cream.

3

NORTH CENTRAL *20301 Oakwood Boulevard, Dearborn, Michigan*

Botsford Inn

HENRY FORD bought and restored this 1836 hostelry, which once served as a stage stop on the line between Detroit and Chicago. Today it maintains a century-old reputation for hospitality combined with delicious meals. Lunch and dinner served every day except Monday. Overnight accommodations.

EGGNOG PIE

For this recipe you will need: 1 envelope plain gelatin, 2 cups milk, 1 tablespoon cornstarch, ¼ teaspoon salt, 6 tablespoons sugar, 2 eggs (separated), 2 teaspoons brandy flavoring, 1 9-inch pie shell, and nutmeg.

Sprinkle gelatin over ¼ cup milk. Mix cornstarch, salt, 3 tablespoons sugar; add remaining milk. Cook in double boiler, stirring, till slightly thickened. Cover; cook 10 minutes more. Add gelatin; stir till dissolved. Beat egg yolks; then add milk mixture. Cook in double boiler 3 minutes, remove from fire, chill till slightly thickened. Beat egg whites till stiff; add remaining sugar, and fold into custard. Flavor. Pour into pie shell; sprinkle with nutmeg. Chill till firm.

PAINTING BY CHARLES W. MOSS

Phil De Graff's Lodges SET amidst 1,200

acres of woods, streams, and lakes, this upper-peninsula resort is open June through November, American plan. Call for
single meal reservations. Winters, owner DeGraff runs Sea
Grape Island Lodge, Box 128, Fort Myers, Florida.

CORNY BISCUITS AU GRATIN

    4 cups Bisquick
    1 teaspoon sugar
   ½ teaspoon salt
    1 heaping tablespoon shortening
     Cheddar cheese (to individual
     taste)
   ½ cup cream-style corn
     Water enough for a soft dough
     Bran
 Mix dry ingredients, then work in

shortening as for pie crust. Grate
cheese into the corn and water, and
mix together into a soft dough. Add
corn-cheese mixture to dry ingredients
and mix fast, adding water as necessary to make a very soft biscuit dough.
"Flour" the board with bran and pat
out dough about ¾ inch thick on top
of it. Cut into biscuits and bake in a
moderately hot oven.

3. **NORTH CENTRAL**

Trout Lake, Michigan

Devon Gables THE charming warmth of this restaurant's English Room, patterned after a small Devonshire Inn, is a striking contrast to its gay Guatemala Room, which achieves a tropical effect with lush indoor gardens. Open for lunch and dinner every day except Monday. Reservations necessary for special parties only.

SPINACH LOAF WITH HORSERADISH SAUCE

1 quart spinach, cooked
1 cup cream sauce
1 cup bread crumbs
3 eggs, separated
2 teaspoons chopped onion
1 tablespoon butter, melted
½ teaspoon salt
⅛ teaspoon pepper

Chop spinach. Mix in other ingredients, folding in beaten egg whites last. Place in pan of hot water and bake in 350° oven for 45 minutes. Excellent for a main course or a vegetable dish.

SAUCE

Fold ¼ cup drained horseradish into ½ pint cream, whipped and sweetened. Add dash of salt.

U. S. 24, Bloomfield Hills, Michigan

NORTH CENTRAL

3

St. Clair Inn

MORE boat tonnage passes by this inn on the St. Clair River than passes through the Suez and Panama Canals combined! Chef Mark Zimmer says he can't recall preparing a menu here that didn't include pickerel. Breakfast, lunch, and dinner served. Overnight accommodations and vacation facilities.

FRIED ST. CLAIR RIVER PICKEREL

Fillet the pickerel, then rinse in cold water and allow it to drain. Sprinkle it with salt and pepper, then dust in flour and paprika (a teaspoon of paprika to every 2 cups flour). Fry the pickerel in a couple of inches of pure rendered lard, adding a little butter, until the fillet is golden brown. Garnish with watercress and parsley, and serve with tartar sauce and lemon slices.

Add parsley, boiled potatoes, and fresh peas; and you have a dish fit for a king.

A Bit of Sweden

A Bit of Sweden FEATURES here are smorgasbord on a natural ice table and decorations of native art pieces. Owner Eric Lundahl often goes back to Sweden just to make sure he hasn't lost touch with Old World recipes and customs. Lunch and dinner except Sunday. Closed during August.

COLLOPS

2¾ pounds round steak (beef)
2 tablespoons butter or fat
¾ tablespoon salt
¾ tablespoon pepper
Allspice
2 bay leaves
1 large onion, sliced
Water or weak stock
2 tablespoons flour
1½ cups cream

Cut beef in 1-inch cubes. Sear on all sides in fat; add seasonings, onion, and enough stock to cover these ingredients. Simmer about 2 hours. Strain and skim the juice in the pan, returning a little of the fat. Add flour mixed with 7 tablespoons water. Stir till browned. Add meat juice gradually. Pour in cream and cook gravy 8 to 10 minutes. Season and pour over meat.

Norton Hotel, 410 Griswold, Detroit, Michigan

NORTH CENTRAL

Pontchartrain Wine Cellars WHEN

Harold Borgman returned from France after World War I, he planted a bit of France in downtown Detroit. Lunch, dinner to 10:00 p.m., except Sundays, holidays. Reservations advisable.

SOUPE A L'OIGNON GRATINEE

4 to 5 pounds short ribs of beef
15 to 20 large onions
¼ cup olive oil
4 tablespoons butter
Salt and pepper
2 tablespoons sugar
French bread or Dutch rusk
Grated Parmesan cheese
Red wine

Simmer beef short ribs in water slowly for 1 hour. Slice onions on the bias—no rings—and sauté in skillet with olive oil. When tender and golden, add butter, salt, pepper, sugar. Remove short ribs from stock and add onions; allow soup to simmer until ready to serve. Cover slice of French bread toast or Dutch rusk with grated Parmesan cheese, and melt under broiler. In each bowl of soup put 1 slice toast and add 1 tablespoon red wine.

3

NORTH CENTRAL

618 Wayne Street, Detroit, Michigan

PAINTING BY A. J. MERIZON

Red Brick Tavern

WHILE a guest in this restful country inn, James Fenimore Cooper wrote *Oak Openings*. Lunch and dinner served every day except Monday. Closed from January 1 through February.

CHOCOLATE ROLL

¾ cup sugar
6 eggs, separated
¼ cup cocoa
¼ cup flour
⅓ teaspoon baking powder
Pinch of salt
½ teaspoon vanilla
1½ cups whipped cream

Add 2 tablespoons sugar to unbeaten egg whites. Add half remaining sugar to yolks; add the rest to the dry ingredients and sift. Beat sugar into yolks; add dry ingredients and vanilla to mixture and beat. Beat whites until stiff and fold in egg yolk mixture. Bake on a cookie sheet covered with heavy wax paper for 20 minutes at 350°. Turn upside down on floured cloth, remove wax paper, and roll. When cool, unroll and spread with whipped cream (sweetened with ¼ cup sugar and 1 teaspoon vanilla). Reroll till ready to cut. Pour chocolate sauce over each portion. Serves 10.

U.S. 131, Plainwell, Michigan

NORTH CENTRAL

3

Boston Oyster House

You needn't go to New England to enjoy sea food, for here is a place furnished and operated in the manner of a traditional seaboard restaurant. Open 11:00 a.m. to midnight. Overnight accommodations.

RED SNAPPER GUMBO

½ pound red snapper, diced
½ onion, diced
½ carrot, diced
½ leek, diced
½ stalk celery, diced
½ cup diced okra
2 tablespoons butter
¼ pound cooked shrimp
2 cups fish stock
1 small can tomatoes
1 tablespoon sherry
Dash of Lea and Perrins sauce
¼ clove garlic, crushed
½ bay leaf
Pinch of chopped parsley
Salt, pepper, and Tabasco sauce

Braise vegetables in butter before adding snapper and shrimp. Continue to braise. Mix remaining ingredients and simmer over slow heat for an hour. Season with salt, pepper, and Tabasco.

Ernest Rickett's RIGHT across from an old land-mark, "the Water Tower," this restaurant has been pleasing patrons since it opened in 1898. It's especially noted for its hearty main courses and variety of desserts. Open 24 hours a day. Reservations necessary.

BROILED STEAK CUBES WITH RED WINE

2 pounds sirloin steak, cubed
24 large mushrooms
1 cup claret or burgundy
1 cup salad oil
2 teaspoons Worcestershire sauce
4 tablespoons catsup
2 tablespoons sugar
2 tablespoons vinegar
1 teaspoon powdered marjoram
1 teaspoon powdered rosemary

Marinate steak cubes and mushrooms for 2 hours in blended wine, salad oil, Worcestershire sauce, catsup, sugar, vinegar, and herbs. Arrange cubes of beef and mushrooms alternately on skewers. Broil, browning well on all sides. Baste frequently with remaining marinade. Serve with grilled tomato and duchess potatoes.

103 East Chicago Avenue, Chicago, Illinois

PAINTING BY CAL DUNN

Pump Room THE late Ernest Byfield's colorful personality was stamped on this place, and today his traditions are being carried on by Jimmy Hart, Pat Hoy, and Gene Barrett, his long-time associates. Lunch and dinner served until 2:00 a.m. Overnight accommodations. Reservations necessary.

GIANT HAWAIIAN PINEAPPLE

¼ fresh pineapple
6 to 8 shrimp or ½ pound lobster
    meat
Olives
Cherries

Cut meat from quartered pineapple in one piece; replace and slice vertically into ½-inch sections. Pull the first out about an inch from the center to the right; the second slice to the left. Alternate all slices in this way. Fill in these spaces with shrimp or lobster as desired. Garnish along the top with pieces of olives and cherries. Chill in refrigerator for at least 30 minutes before serving. Serve with a side dish of sauce for the shrimp or lobster. Serves 1.

3

NORTH CENTRAL   *Hotel Ambassador East, Chicago, Illinois*
154

The Pantry IN spring blazing Holland tulips encircle this restaurant, but any time you'll see crowds of gourmets there. Lunch, dinner, except Monday and Tuesday. Reservations advisable. Closed January 2 to last Saturday in January.

BLITZ TORTE

¾ cup butter
¾ cup sugar
6 egg yolks
1½ cups cake flour
1½ teaspoons baking powder
½ cup milk

Cream butter and sugar together thoroughly; add beaten egg yolks. Sift cake flour and baking powder into mixture alternately with milk. Pour into 2 9-inch layer-cake pans and spread following mixture on each:

6 beaten egg whites

718 Garden Street, Park Ridge, Illinois

1½ cups sifted sugar
1 cup walnuts, chopped
Bake for 45 minutes in 350° oven.

FILLING

2 eggs, beaten
1½ cups milk
1½ teaspoons cornstarch
1¾ tablespoons sugar
1 teaspoon vanilla

Stir over medium fire until mixture thickens and boils. Place bottom layer meringue-side down, top layer meringue-side up; spread filling between.

NORTH CENTRAL 3

The Brick House FOUR dining rooms (three with cheery fireplaces) and good, home-cooked food make eating at this pleasant 1870 house a most satisfying experience. Lunch and dinner served every day except Saturday.

ORANGE RAISIN CAKE

    1 cup brown sugar
    1 egg
    ½ cup butter
    1 cup buttermilk
    2 cups flour
    1 teaspoon soda
    1 teaspoon baking powder
    Pinch of salt
    1 orange, juice and rind
    ½ cup raisins
    ½ cup nutmeats

Beat sugar, egg, butter, and buttermilk together. Add flour, soda, baking powder, and salt. Grind together orange rind, raisins, and nuts. Add half of ground mixture to batter. Mix, pour into cake tin, and bake 40 minutes at 350°. Pour juice of orange over cake as soon as tin is removed from oven. Add remaining ground mixture to a powdered sugar icing and spread over cake.

NORTH CENTRAL

402 Lincolnway West, Morrison, Illinois

Fanny's

IN 1946 Mrs. Ray Lazzar, better known as "Fanny," started out with meager capital and a tiny restaurant. Today she can boast that notables from all over the world have enjoyed dinner in her candlelit dining room. Dinner served from 5:00 p.m. to 10:00 p.m. daily and from noon to 10:00 p.m. on Sunday. Closed on Monday and Christmas Day.

FANNY'S SALAD DRESSING

Oil	Tomato paste
Tarragon vinegar	Orange juice
Chutney	Ground pecans
Brown sugar	Garlic
Salt and pepper	Onions
Mustard	Celery
Fresh tomatoes	Parsley

Despite wheedling offers of up to $10,000 for her recipes, Fanny will give only the ingredients used in her salad dressing. It's up to you to figure out the amounts! The true detective will buy a pint bottle at the restaurant and have it analyzed.

1601 Simpson Street, Evanston, Illinois

Klas' Restaurant

HERE it's easy to imagine you're in Bohemia, for everything suggests an Old World café —from string orchestra to succulent Czech dishes. Open from 11:00 a.m. to 1:00 a.m. every day except Monday.

BOHEMIAN KOLACKY

1 cake compressed yeast
1 cup scalded milk, lukewarm
1 tablespoon sugar
½ cup sugar
½ cup softened lard
2 small eggs, well beaten
1 teaspoon salt
3 cups all-purpose flour
1 cup cooked prune pulp
2 tablespoons melted margarine
¼ teaspoon ground cloves

Combine yeast, milk, and tablespoon of sugar. Let stand while creaming ¼ cup sugar and softened lard together. Add eggs and salt to creamed mixture, blending well. Stir in yeast mixture, alternating with flour. Beat well, let rise until doubled in bulk. Shape into small rolls. Make indentation in center of each roll and fill with a spoonful of prune pulp to which margarine, cloves, and remaining sugar have been added. Let rise until light, about 10 minutes, and bake in a hot (400°) oven for about 15 minutes, or until done. Makes about 15 tarts.

5734 West Cermak Road, Cicero, Illinois

Well-of-the-Sea

THIS is a strange and wonderful new restaurant devoted almost exclusively to sea food. The unusual interior gives you the feeling that you are eating on the floor of the ocean. The late Ernest Byfield founded it. Open for lunch and dinner. Overnight accommodations in the hotel.

CRABMEAT IN SKILLET

4 ounces crabmeat, lump style
½ ounce butter
1 teaspoon tarragon vinegar
Dash of Lea and Perrins
⅛ ounce chopped chives
Freshly ground black pepper and salt to taste

Heat butter in skillet until it is very hot, but not burned. Add crabmeat and sauté; add vinegar and dash of Lea and Perrins. Finally add chives and salt and pepper to your taste. Cover the skillet and remove from heat. Serve immediately. This recipe is for a single portion.

Hotel Sherman, Chicago, Illinois

NORTH CENTRAL 3

The Covered Wagon   THIS eating place in the bustling Loop breathes the spirit of the West from the interior design to the he-man specialties like steak, wall-eyed pike, and pheasant with wild rice. Lunch and dinner served to 1:00 a.m. every day except Sunday and holidays.

DOMESTICATED RING-NECK PHEASANT WITH WILD RICE

Clean pheasant; split it down both sides of backbone. (Use backbone and neck in stock pot.) Split down breastbone, making two halves. Wipe thoroughly with clean dry cloth. Season well with salt and pepper; dust with flour. Fry in hot fat until golden brown. Make a thin, well-seasoned sauce of stock and cream (one part of each). Put pheasant in a pot, cover with cream sauce, put on slow fire, and simmer. When almost done, add about 1 ounce of sherry. Serve with wild rice.

Steam ½ cup rice until tender and fluffy. Put in colander to drain and cool. Chop ½ onion and about 3 strips bacon; sauté in a frying pan until brown; now add rice. Season with salt and pepper. Thoroughly heat on a quick hot fire.

PAINTING BY C. F. KORTEN

Urbana-Lincoln Hotel IN this modern hotel the Lincoln Dining Room is hung with paintings by the art faculty of the University of Illinois. Breakfast, lunch, and dinner. Overnight accommodations.

STUFFED MUSHROOMS

12 large mushrooms
1 tablespoon lemon juice
4 tablespoons butter
1 cup minced white meat of chicken
1 cup fresh bread crumbs
Chicken broth
1 egg
1 teaspoon minced parsley
1 tablespoon grated onion
1 teaspoon salt
¼ teaspoon pepper

Remove mushroom stems; place caps in cold water to which lemon has been added to prevent discoloration. Chop stems into fine pieces; sauté in butter. Add chicken, stirring to prevent burning. Moisten some bread crumbs with chicken broth and egg; add to mixture. Stir in parsley, grated onion, salt, and pepper. Stuff mushroom caps and sprinkle with buttered crumbs. Bake 30 to 45 minutes in shallow pan with a little water. Serves 6.

209 South Broadway, Urbana, Illinois

Fallhall Glen

Fallhall Glen THIS summer resort on the banks of a rushing trout steam is a perfect spot for a peaceful vacation in the outdoors. Breakfast, lunch, and dinner served. Overnight accommodations and vacation facilities. Reservations necessary. Open May 1 to November 1.

CHEESE BEANS A LA FALLHALL

2 cans cut yellow wax beans
   Butter
   Brown sugar
   White sauce
½ cup grated cheese
½ cup aged cheese

Drain some juice from beans and cook in a little butter and brown sugar until dry. Combine with a white sauce flavored with ½ cup grated cheese. Place in a buttered casserole dish and cover the top with ½ cup ground aged cheese. Bake 20 minutes in a moderate oven. (To age cheese: dry cheese, grate it until very fine, and pack in glass jars. It keeps indefinitely and has a fine tang.) Most guests at the Glen do not consider their vacation complete without at least one serving of this delicacy.

R. R. 5, Black River Falls, Wisconsin

Brad Ryan's Lake Breeze Lodge NEAR

Nicolet National Forest, this vacation spot is set on sixty lake-front acres. Vegetables and fruit come from surrounding gardens daily. Breakfast, lunch, and dinner. Overnight accommodations and vacation facilities. Reservations necessary. Open May 15 to September 15.

SOUTHERN PECAN PIE

2 cups pecans
2 cups brown corn syrup
1 cup white sugar
½ pound butter
6 eggs
2 unbaked pie shells
Whipped cream

Boil sugar, syrup, and butter together. Beat eggs, then blend with hot syrup mixture slowly as you continue to beat. Divide mixture evenly between pie shells and sprinkle with pecans. Bake in 350° oven for 20 minutes and for 15 minutes at 400°. Pies will crack slightly and be jelly-like. Serve with collar of whipped cream.

County Trunk X, Three Lakes, Wisconsin

PAINTING BY CHARLES W. MOSS

Fish Shanty   THIS eating place began as a modest sandwich counter connected with the century-old Smith Brothers' commercial fishery. Today it has expanded to block length and serves thousands annually. Lunch and dinner served 11:30 a.m. to 9:00 p.m. every day, except Thanksgiving Day and Christmas Day. Only fish meals served.

FISH LOAF

2 cups flaked cooked fish
1½ cups bread crumbs
½ teaspoon baking powder
⅔ cup chopped celery
⅓ cup chopped onion
1 tablespoon lemon juice
1 cup milk
1 tablespoon minced pimento
1 tablespoon chopped green
    pepper
Salt and pepper

Mix ingredients and form loaf in an oiled loaf pan. Bake in moderate oven (350°) until brown and firm. Serve with desired cream sauce. This is a recipe guaranteed to make your family fish eaters!

3

NORTH CENTRAL

Port Washington, Wisconsin

PAINTING BY CAL DUNN

Mader's Famous Restaurant BACK in

1902 when Charles Mader, a German immigrant, founded this establishment, he charged 20 cents for a steak dinner and a nickel for two glasses of beer. Prices have changed a bit but not the high cooking standards. Open 11:00 a.m. to 8:30 p.m.

KOENIGSBERGER KLOPS WITH CAPER SAUCE (Meat Balls)

To make meat balls, mix together ½ pound each ground lamb, veal, and pork. Add 1 small can sardines (chopped), 2 green onions with tops (chopped), pinch each salt and pepper. Soak ½ small loaf white bread (crust removed) in milk; add to meat along with 2 egg whites and mix well. Form into balls the size of golf balls. Cook in and serve with Caper Sauce.

CAPER SAUCE

Brown 2 tablespoons butter and 3 tablespoons flour in a sauce kettle. Add 1 quart cold water and mix till smooth. Let boil; then turn down flame. Put in meat balls; simmer 15 to 20 minutes. Add ¼ cup capers, 2 beaten egg yolks, ½ glass Rhine wine, ½ cup cream; simmer till meat balls are done. Serve with noodles.

1037-41 North Third Street, Milwaukee, Wisconsin   **NORTH CENTRAL**

Lowell Inn FOR 98 years this serene and beautiful country inn has been noted for its excellent food. Breakfast, lunch, and dinner, every day except Monday. Overnight accommodations and vacation facilities. Reservations necessary.

BROOK TROUT AU BLEU

Poach the fish 4 to 5 minutes, depending on its size, in a court-bouillon made by boiling bones of other fish in water, then removing them to add either lemon juice or white wine, a spice bag, a vegetable bag, and salt. Remove the trout, which has turned a beautiful blue color, to a fish plate, and garnish with finger cucumber sandwiches and water cress.

FINGER CUCUMBER SANDWICHES

Slice cucumbers very thin, salt down, and let stand ½ hour. Squeeze out the juice; add lemon, finely cut onion, and a little thick cream. Spread between sandwich bread, cut into finger shapes.

Lutsen Resort

Lutsen Resort OPEN the year round, this Lake Superior inn was one of the first resorts in the state. It offers a full schedule of summer sports as well as some of the Midwest's best skiing in the winter. Breakfast, lunch, and dinner served. Overnight accommodations and vacation facilities.

SWEDISH RYE BREAD

2 cups dark rye flour
10 cups white flour
2½ cups lukewarm water
2 cakes compressed yeast
1 cup molasses
1 cup brown sugar

2 tablespoons salt

Knead ingredients and let rise overnight. Shape into 6 loaves and let rise double in bulk. Bake 45 minutes in a moderate oven. Each loaf will cut into about 10 slices.

The Fox and Hounds   HOSTS of this inn are Alta and Ray Wolf, an artist. Lunch and dinner, except Mondays in winter. Recreation facilities. Reservations.

ICEBOX CHEESE TORTE

1 pound cottage cheese
⅓ cup cold water
2 tablespoons gelatin
2 eggs, separated
1 cup sugar
½ teaspoon salt
½ cup milk
½ tablespoon vanilla
½ pint heavy cream, whipped
CRUST
18 graham crackers, rolled fine
⅓ cup sugar
⅓ cup melted butter
½ teaspoon cinnamon

Pour cold water in mixing bowl and sprinkle with gelatin. Beat egg yolks lightly; add ½ cup sugar, salt, and then milk. Cook over boiling water until custard-like, stirring occasionally while cooking. Add gelatin to hot mixture and stir until well dissolved. Cool until mixture begins to thicken, then add cheese and vanilla. Beat until smooth. Whip cream, egg whites, and ½ cup sugar. Fold both into cheese mixture. Line 2-inch deep pan with crust mixture and pour cheese mixture over it. Set in refrigerator. Serve chilled.

3

NORTH CENTRAL   *6 miles w. of Richfield on State 167, Hubertus, Wis.*

168

Grecian Gardens

FOR 40 years Jim Mertikas has been delighting patrons with Greek specialties. Open for lunch and dinner from 11:00 a.m. to 1:00 a.m.

GREEK DALMADES

2 cups rice, uncooked
1 onion
1 celery heart
3 sprigs parsley
2 pounds choice ground beef
2 eggs
   Grape leaves or cooked cabbage leaves
¼ pound butter
1 quart water
1 pinch nutmeg
   Salt and pepper to taste

Boil rice. Chop onion, celery, and parsley; and mix with beef. Season and add cooked rice and eggs. Make 1½-inch meat balls out of mixture and wrap in grape leaves or cooked cabbage leaves. Place in pot with butter and water, and boil over slow fire for ½ hour.

SAUCE

3 egg yolks
1 tablespoon cornstarch
2 tablespoons water
   Juice of 3 lemons

Combine these ingredients with juice from dalmades and pour over wrapped meat balls before serving. Serves 8.

205 South Sixth Street, St. Louis, Missouri

SOUTH CENTRAL 4

PAINTING BY CHARLES BANKS WILSON

Big Spring Inn

THE name comes from a spring which originates in the city park, flows across the street in front of this inn, and forms a trout pool in the yard. Breakfast, lunch, dinner served daily. Overnight, vacation facilities.

HAPPY DAY CAKE

½ cup shortening
1¼ cups sugar
2 eggs, unbeaten
2½ cups cake flour
3 teaspoons baking powder
¼ teaspoon salt
1 cup milk
1 teaspoon vanilla
6 ounces semi-sweet chocolate chips

Cream shortening and sugar. Add eggs one at a time and beat well. Sift flour, baking powder, and salt. Add to mixture in 3 portions, alternating with milk. Add vanilla. Pour half of batter into greased and floured 9-inch cake pan. Melt half of chocolate chips and add to remaining batter. Then stir in unmelted chips. Pour this batter into a second greased and floured 9-inch cake pan. Bake 30 minutes at 375°. When cool, ice with a chocolate butter cream icing.

SOUTH CENTRAL

S. of U.S. 60 at 320 W. Spring St., Neosho, Mo.

Edmonds A touch of New England in the West is this restaurant furnished in early American style and specializing in Maine lobster and sea food. Open from 11:00 a.m. to midnight, every day except Sunday and Christmas Day.

EGGPLANT PROVENCALE

1 medium-size eggplant, peeled and sliced
4 large tomatoes, peeled and chopped
½ cup olive oil
2 cloves garlic, crushed
½ cup bread crumbs
½ cup Parmesan cheese
Salt and pepper, to taste
Simmer tomato with 3 tablespoons olive oil in a skillet until it thickens. Heat remaining olive oil in another skillet before mixing in combined garlic, crumbs, and cheese. Dredge salted eggplant slices in crumb mixture and fry until tender in oil; then remove to casserole. Put tomato sauce and crumb mixture between layers, and spread on top also. Bake for 30 minutes. Good, hot or cold.

Arrow Rock Tavern

Arrow Rock Tavern THIS hostelry adjoining a state park has been in operation since the building was erected in 1830. Open for breakfast, lunch, and dinner. Overnight accommodations and vacation facilities. Reservations necessary.

SCALLOPED EGGPLANT

1 large eggplant
2 tablespoons butter
1 can mushroom soup
½ cup bread crumbs
1 teaspoon sugar
3 tablespoons grated cheese

Slice eggplant and soak in salt water; drain and drop in boiling water. Cook until tender. Arrange in layers in buttered baking dish, dot with butter, and pour can of mushroom soup over it. Sprinkle with bread crumbs, sugar, and cheese. Bake in medium oven for 30 minutes.

Arrow Rock, Missouri

PAINTING BY JESSIE H. RICKLY

Hotel Taneycomo

DELICIOUS meals cooked by Ozark mountain women have distinguished this resort and brought vacationists back year after year. Breakfast, lunch, and dinner served. Closed from middle of September to the middle of May. Overnight accommodations in the main building or in lakeshore cabins. Vacation facilities.

OZARK BAKELESS PUDDING

½ cup butter
1 cup sugar
2 eggs
1 cup chopped nut meats
1 small can crushed pineapple
  (peaches may be substituted)
½ pound graham crackers

Cream butter and sugar; add well-beaten eggs, nuts, and pineapple. Crush crackers; then alternate layers of crackers and mixture in a dish. Set for 12 hours in cooling room or refrigerator. Serve with whipped cream topping or an orange sauce. Serves 6.

Rockaway Beach, Missouri

SOUTH CENTRAL 4

Hotel Cornhusker

FOOD from all over the United States is served here; especially popular is their salad with garlic bread. Breakfast, lunch, dinner until 1:00 a.m. Overnight accommodations.

CORNHUSKER SALAD

Break crisp head lettuce into small pieces. Add sliced radishes, cucumber, a quartered tomato, julienne-cut green pepper, celery, carrots, green onions, and fresh watercress. Mix these ingredients with olive oil dressing (below) and top salad bowl with anchovy fillets, capers, and quartered hard-boiled egg. Serve with garlic bread.

SPECIAL OLIVE OIL DRESSING

5 ounces sugar

2 ounces salt
1 teaspoon dry mustard
2 cloves garlic, crushed
½ cup green onion, chopped fine
1 tablespoon Worcestershire sauce
1½ pints wine vinegar
1 quart olive oil
Juice of 3 lemons

Mix dry ingredients in bowl. Add oil and whip well. Add remaining ingredients. Makes about 3 quarts.

SOUTH CENTRAL

301 S. Thirteenth Street, Lincoln, Nebraska

Hotel Sam Peck A COMFORTABLE hotel, run by
Mr. and Mrs. Sam Peck, which has been noted for years both
for its excellent food and attractive interior design. Open for
breakfast, lunch, and dinner. Overnight accommodations.

ESCALLOPED CHICKEN

1 large boiled hen, cut into pieces
1 pound fresh mushrooms
1 stalk celery
4 cups rich cream sauce
1 teaspoon grated onion
  Pinch of red pepper
  Salt and pepper to taste
  Cracker crumbs
  Butter

Saute' mushrooms and celery; then
add the cream sauce. Follow this with
chicken, onion, salt, and pepper. Place
a layer of this mixture in a large, shallow baking dish, cover with a layer of
cracker crumbs and spots of butter, and
repeat process until the dish is filled.
Serves 6 persons.

Crescent Hotel PERCHED on the crest of one of the Ozark mountains, this resort hotel in the old tradition is surrounded by the hilly town of Eureka Springs. Breakfast, lunch, and dinner served. Overnight accommodations and vacation facilities. Closed November 15 to April 1.

HUCKLEBERRY MUFFINS

1 cup huckleberries
2 cups flour
¼ teaspoon salt
⅓ cup shortening
4 teaspoons baking powder
1 cup milk
1 egg

Wash and drain huckleberries and sprinkle with ½ teaspoon flour. Sift dry ingredients and cut in shortening. To this add milk and beaten egg. Stir floured berries in quickly; don't mash them. Bake in hot greased muffin pans for 20 minutes in a moderate oven. (Blueberries can be substituted.) Pop a batch into the oven for a Sunday morning breakfast surprise.

Crescent Park, Eureka Springs, Arkansas

The Boulevard Room THE kitchen in the Hotel Jefferson is presided over by Chef Mauclair, noted for curry dishes. Lunch, dinner, and supper. Overnight accommodations.

RICE MANGALAIS WITH CURRY SAUCE

1½ cups rice, uncooked
2 onions, chopped fine
1 clove garlic
2 teaspoons curry powder
¼ pound currants
¼ pound almonds, chopped
3½ cups chicken broth
Salt and pepper to taste

Braise onions and add garlic and rice. Cook for 1 minute. Stir in curry powder, currants, almonds, and chicken broth. Bake in moderate oven for 18 minutes. Serves 10.

CURRY SAUCE

2½ tablespoons curry powder
3 onions, chopped
1 cup diced ham
2 apples, diced
2 tablespoons flour
1½ quarts chicken broth

Mix all ingredients together. Strain and season to taste. Cook for ½ hour and serve with Rice Mangalais.

415 North 12th Boulevard, St. Louis, Missouri

PAINTING BY C. F. KORTEN

Angelo's ANGELO XIDIS, owner and chef at this famous spot, had one hard-and-fast rule: Never reveal a recipe. His secrets were successfully kept before we coaxed this one from him. Open for breakfast, lunch, and dinner 7:00 a.m. to 10:00 p.m., except Christmas Day.

ANGELO'S BROILED FLOUNDER AND SAUCE

Make several small cuts across the top of the cleaned fish and insert slices of garlic. Sprinkle fish with oregano and broil. Make a sauce by combining lemon juice, a touch of mustard, mayonnaise, olive oil, chopped capers, parsley, and salt and pepper. Pour sauce over broiled fish and heat in oven for a few minutes before serving.

Sounds simple, but Angelo takes it for granted that you will know the exact amounts to use.

4 **SOUTH CENTRAL**
178

3206 West Beach, Gulfport, Mississippi

PAINTING BY JOSEPH DONALDSON

Old Southern Tea Room

WAITRESSES in costume serve such delicacies as shrimp gumbo, fried chicken, hot biscuits. Salads and cakes are made in owner Mary McKay's home kitchen by her own cook. Breakfast, lunch, dinner daily, 6:30 a.m. to 9:30 p.m., except Christmas Day.

STUFFED BELL PEPPER CREOLE

8 medium bell peppers
1 button garlic
2 onions, chopped
½ stick butter
½ cup each: tomato juice, water
1 small can tomatoes
½ cup chopped ham
2 cups cracker crumbs
1 egg, well beaten
½ teaspoon sugar

Wash and chop 2 peppers (leave in seeds), garlic, and onions. Cook in butter in skillet till tender. Add tomato juice, water, tomatoes, ham, and cook till these sink to bottom of pan. Remove from fire; add crumbs and egg. Scald remaining peppers with sugar and little salt; then stuff with filling. Sprinkle crumbs over top, brush with melted butter and paprika. Bake 20 minutes at 350°. Serves 6.

1201 Monroe Street, Vicksburg, Mississippi

SOUTH CENTRAL

Antoine's

ONE of the world's famous restaurants since 1840, this romantic spot is now run by the founder's grandson with the same high-quality cuisine. Lunch and dinner noon to 9:00 p.m., except Sundays.

FRENCH PANCAKES A LA GELEE

½ cup sifted all-purpose flour
1 egg
1 egg yolk
⅛ teaspoon salt
5 tablespoons milk
   (approximately)
3 tablespoons currant or red
   raspberry jelly
Powdered sugar

Combine flour, egg, egg yolk, salt, and milk. Beat with rotary beater until smooth. If necessary, add more milk to make batter the consistency of light cream. Cover; chill for ½ hour in refrigerator. Heat heavy iron skillet; wipe out with waxed paper which has been dipped in butter. Pour in enough batter to barely cover bottom of skillet, tipping while adding batter. Brown pancakes on both sides. Remove from skillet; spread with jelly; roll up jelly-roll fashion. Sprinkle with a little powdered sugar. Place under broiler to glaze. Serve immediately. Yields 12 to 15 5-inch pancakes.

Tarpon Inn

SITUATED in one of the world's most famous fishing resorts, this unofficial tarpon fishing capital of the world gives the sportsmen who flock here a good lesson in how to prepare their haul. Breakfast, lunch, and dinner. Overnight accommodations (American plan), recreation facilities. Open March 1 to around January 1. Reservations necessary.

SEA-FOOD COCKTAIL SAUCE

1 cup tomato catsup
2 tablespoons vinegar
Few drops Tabasco sauce
1 tablespoon horseradish
½ cup mayonnaise
1 teaspoon lemon juice
1 teaspoon Lea and Perrins sauce

Mix ingredients in order listed and blend well. Chill before serving. For variation, the Tabasco sauce, vinegar, and mayonnaise may be omitted. Also some people prefer sauce made with only 2 teaspoons mayonnaise instead of ½ cup. Makes 6 average servings.

Port Aransas, Mustang Island, Texas

Granger's THIS is a "must stop" for a sea-food lover, for the menu is limited exclusively to fish and shellfish. Open from noon to 9:00 p.m. every day except Monday. Reservations advisable on week ends. Closed during December.

TARTAR SAUCE

> 1 tablespoon sour pickles
> 1 tablespoon dill pickles
> 1 tablespoon parsley
> 1 tablespoon green olives
> 1 tablespoon chives
> ½ cup mayonnaise
> Chop pickles, parsley, olives, and

chives into fine pieces. Drain or even wring these ingredients in a clean cloth to prevent mixture from curdling due to excess vinegar. Combine with mayonnaise, preferably homemade with an olive-oil base. Serve with your favorite fish.

SOUTH CENTRAL

Sabine Pass, Texas

PAINTING BY ALOIS FABRY, JR.

Shamrock Hotel A POPULAR dining spot in Glenn McCarthy's fabulous hotel is the Aquatic Terrace—a splash away from the giant outdoor swimming pool. Breakfast, lunch, dinner. Overnight accommodations and recreation facilities.

CREAMED CHICKEN HONGROISE

1 5- to 6-pound hen
2 carrots
2 stalks celery
1 leek
1½ ounces salt
4 onions, medium size
2 shallots
1 ounce butter
1 teaspoon paprika
1 ounce flour
½ pint milk
½ cup cream

Cover chicken with water; bring to a boil. Add carrots, 3 onions, celery, leek, and salt. Cook 2 hours. Remove from pan and strain stock through cheese cloth. Bone fowl and cut into small pieces. Chop 1 onion and shallots and add to melted butter; cook until slightly brown. Add paprika and flour. Stir and cook for 5 minutes; slowly pour in stock and boiling milk. Season to taste. Add fowl and boiling cream. Bring mixture to a boil. Serves 8.

South Main at Holcombe, Houston, Texas

SOUTH CENTRAL 4

183

Original Mexican Restaurant

AROUND the corner from the Alamo, this is the oldest Mexican restaurant in the United States. Open 11:00 a.m. to 9:00 p.m.

BEEF TACO

2 pounds ground round steak
1 teaspoon cooking oil
1 tablespoon chopped onion
Dash of garlic
½ teaspoon ground comino seeds
½ teaspoon oregano
½ teaspoon hot green chili pepper
Dash of pepper
⅓ teaspoon salt
½ cup tomato sauce

Boil round steak in water. When cooked, add and mix in the other ingredients to make the stuffing for tortillas.

TORTILLA

2 cups tamalina (cornmeal)
1 tablespoon salt
Lard, to crumble

Mix dry ingredients with lard and enough water to make the dough thin. Roll out to ⅛ inch thickness and cut about the size of a saucer. For frying tortillas, use sufficient oil or fat to float them in the pan. Double them over once during frying and cook until crisp. Stuff each tortilla with several tablespoons of meat mixture; top with shredded lettuce and salad dressing.

SOUTH CENTRAL

115-121 Losoya Street, San Antonio, Texas

Bill Wood's Famous Foods

JUST five minutes from the business district, this restaurant has the true Western atmosphere of the ranch house. Open from 6:00 a.m. to 11:00 p.m. Overnight accommodations and vacation facilities are available.

BARBECUED SPARERIBS

To serve about 20 persons, you will need 10 pounds of spareribs. First prepare a dry base with:

5 tablespoons celery salt
2 tablespoons red pepper
½ cup salt
2 ounces comino seeds, ground
½ cup black pepper

Mix these ingredients together. Before applying to the spareribs, rub the meat on all sides with vinegar. When the meat is sufficiently moist, the powdered mixture should be rubbed in carefully. Cook the spareribs over an open fire, preferably with hickory wood used as logs. The barbecuing process will take 2 to 3 hours, depending upon the intensity of the fire.

At the Circle, Waco, Texas

SOUTH CENTRAL

PAINTING BY HARRY BORGMAN

Kelley's OWNER George Kelley raises his own steaks, pork chops, and turkey dinners on his 3,000-acre ranch at Hempstead, Texas. Open for lunch and dinner every day.

KELLEY'S SPECIAL SALAD DRESSING

1 pint mayonnaise
2 hard-boiled eggs, chopped fine
3 ounces vinegar
2 teaspoonfuls horseradish
2 teaspoonfuls Worcestershire sauce
1 clove garlic, ground
½ teaspoon paprika

Mix the above ingredients together and place in a tight-lidded jar until ready to use. The recipe makes approximately a quart of dressing.

910 Texas, Houston, Texas

Casa de Palmas Hotel

SURROUNDED by palms, rubber trees, and colorful poinsettias, this hotel is reminiscent of old Mexico. Breakfast, lunch, dinner served to 9:00 p.m. Overnight accommodations in the main building or bungalows with flower-filled patios. Vacation facilities.

SLICED BREAST OF TURKEY MORNAY ON TOAST

3 slices turkey
1 pint milk
4 ounces butter
2 tablespoons flour
½ teaspoon salt
2 ounces American cheese
1 egg yolk
Grated cheese

Boil milk and add melted butter, flour, salt, and cheese. Simmer 5 minutes and stir in egg yolk before removing from fire. Cut 3 slices of toast into triangles and place a large slice of turkey on each, then cover with sauce. Sprinkle with grated cheese and brown in oven. Chef Freada Rougeot serves this dish with buttered asparagus tips and Saratoga potatoes.

113 North Main Street, McAllen, Texas

SOUTH CENTRAL

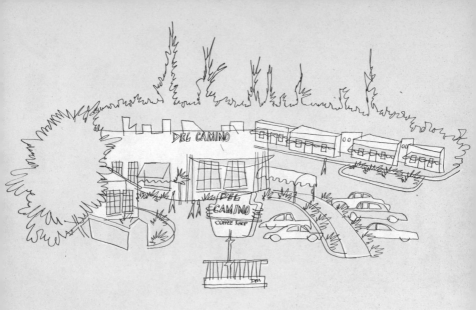

Del Camino Coffee Shop NATIONALLY renowned steaks are featured here. Breakfast, lunch, and dinner. Overnight accommodations; motor courts.

JAM CAKE

1 cup sugar	½ cup butter
½ cup sweet milk	2 cups flour

1 teaspoon baking soda
3 eggs, beaten

2 cups jam	2 glasses jelly

1 teaspoon cinnamon
1 teaspoon allspice
1 teaspoon nutmeg
1 teaspoon cloves
1 teaspoon ginger

Cream sugar and butter. Add milk alternately with flour, which has been sifted with soda. Add all other ingredients and combine, being careful not to break jam and jelly into too-small pieces. Bake in 9-inch layers and fill with pecan whip.

PECAN WHIP

1½ cups Texas pecans
3 cups sugar
1 cup whipping cream
1 tablespoon butter

Combine 2 cups sugar, cream, and butter. Melt remaining sugar in a warm skillet, until brown, but do not burn. When sugar is melted, add other mixture and cook until heavy. Remove from fire and beat until creamy. Add pecans and put cake together.

SOUTH CENTRAL

U.S. 80 East, El Paso, Texas

Baldpate Inn

IN addition to their collection of over 12,000 keys, owners Mr. and Mrs. Gordon Mace possess a breathtaking view of Estes Park. Breakfast, lunch, and dinner served every day. Overnight accommodations and vacation facilities. Closed September 10 to June 10. Reservations necessary.

TUNA NOODLE CASSEROLE

1 can tuna fish
1 pound noodles
1 small onion, sliced thin
1 can mushroom soup
    Pepper to taste
    Pinch of thyme
1 small package potato chips, crushed

Cook noodles in boiling, salted water. Sauté onion in butter until a light brown. Place half of the noodles in casserole, and spread with layer of onion slices, tuna fish, and mushroom soup. Top with remainder of noodles, sprinkle with pepper and thyme, and cover with chips. Bake in 325° oven about 30 minutes until thick and brown.

State Highway 7, Estes Park, Colorado

PAINTING BY EDGAR BRITTON

Stagecoach Inn

AT the foot of Pikes Peak and near the entrance to historic Ute Pass, this restaurant is famous for its mountain trout and Colorado cherry pie. Lunch and dinner daily except Monday. Closed September 5 to May 26.

CHERRY PIE

2 cups fresh Colorado cherries, pitted
1 tablespoon flour
1½ cups sugar
2 rich pastry pie crusts
1 tablespoon butter

Mix flour and sugar, then stir in with cherries. Pour into pastry shell, dot with butter, and cover with pastry top. Bake slowly for 45 minutes in a 350° oven.

RICH PASTRY PIE CRUST
2½ cups sifted flour
1 teaspoon salt
¾ cup shortening
¼ cup water

Mix flour and salt. Cut shortening into it until pieces are size of a bean. Mix well with water until dough comes together and can be shaped into a ball. Divide into 2 parts and roll out crusts. Makes two 9-inch pie crusts.

702 Manitou Avenue (U.S. 24), Manitou Springs, Colorado

The Country Kitchen COLONEL and Mrs.

Hudson's smorgasbord table is heavily laden with delicacies, and fine food is served in a beautiful dining room. Dinner only, daily except Monday. Closed October 1 to March 31.

GREEN RICE

1½ cups rice, cooked
2 tablespoons finely chopped onion
¼ teaspoon minced garlic
3 tablespoons olive oil or butter
½ cup ground or finely chopped parsley
1 cup milk
1 teaspoon salt
1 teaspoon Worcestershire sauce
1 cup grated cheddar cheese
2 eggs, slightly beaten

Sauté chopped onion and minced garlic in olive oil or butter. Measure cooked rice and ground parsley into a mixing bowl; then add milk, salt, Worcestershire sauce, cheddar cheese, and slightly beaten eggs.

Add sautéed onion and garlic; mix thoroughly and pour mixture into buttered baking dish. Bake in a moderate oven (350°) for about 40 minutes. Serves 6.

U.S. 85, Littleton, Colorado

Riverside Lodge and Ranch LOCATED
on the banks of the South St. Vrain River, this resort is 12 miles
up St. Vrain Canyon, the most scenic route to Estes Park. Breakfast, lunch, and dinner; chuck wagon dinner every Thursday
evening. Overnight accommodations and vacation facilities.
Open June 15 to September 15.

CHUCK WAGON DINNER

An hour before mealtime a huge pile
of hay, placed over charcoal, is burned
to a bed of glowing coals. Ears of sweet
corn with the green husk left on are
placed in the coals and are turned until the husks are charred (about 15
minutes). These are kept hot while the
inch-thick T-bone steaks are broiled on
the fire. Meanwhile a 50-cup coffee pot
is simmering on the coals and the
baked beans and cowboy biscuits
(made like regular biscuits and cut
with 3-inch biscuit cutter) are baking
in the Dutch oven. This is served with
a fresh mountain-grown vegetable salad, preserves, pickles, and dessert.

WEST

State Highway 7, Lyons, Colorado

PAINTING BY EDGAR BRITTON

Indian Grill

AUTHENTIC Indian relics, collected in the area, decorate this popular restaurant, which is located in the center of Colorado Springs. Open for lunch and dinner, except Tuesday.

POACHED COLORADO RAINBOW TROUT

½ pound trout per person

COURT BOUILLON
    7 quarts water
    4 ounces salt
    ½ pint vinegar
    5 ounces carrots
    5 ounces onions
    Sprig of parsley
    ½ bay leaf

Sprig of thyme
½ ounce coarsely ground peppercorns

Place trout in heavy iron kettle and cover with Court Bouillon, which has been prepared beforehand. Boil gently (rapid boiling will break fish) 15 minutes. Remove trout and serve with melted butter.

27 East Pikes Peak Avenue, Colorado Springs, Colorado

WEST 5

Challenger Inn

AN ideal climate the year round makes this spot popular as a summer and winter resort, though you most probably think of it in connection with skiing. Breakfast, lunch, and dinner. Overnight accommodations and vacation facilities. Closed October 15 to December 19.

STUFFED IDAHO MOUNTAIN TROUT SAUTE ALMANDINE

Clean fresh Idaho mountain trout. Trim off fins and take out backbone, being careful not to cut through back skin. Take ½ pound salmon meat, ½ pound halibut meat, 1 ounce of onion, 1 garlic bead and run through buffalo chopper till very fine. To this add 3 egg yolks, 1 cup cream, 2 tablespoons fresh bread crumbs. Then add salt and pepper, Lea and Perrins sauce, cayenne pepper, and lemon juice to taste. Fill trout with this stuffing, roll in flour, and fry in olive oil till golden brown on each side. Finish cooking in 375° oven.

Sauté a few almonds in butter. Add lemon juice. When almonds are brown, add chopped parsley. Serve this sauce hot with fish.

Sun Valley, Idaho

El Rancho Cordova

NATIVE Mexican dishes served by waitresses in gay costumes make this like a bit of old Mexico. Open for dinner from 5:30 p.m. to 11:00 p.m., except Monday. Reservations necessary. Closed during August.

ALBONDIGAS SOUP A LA CORDOVA

For a tangy Mexican touch to your meals, try the recipe of a famous restaurant which specializes in south-of-the-border recipes. For this soup mix 1 pound lean beef (cut into small pieces), 1 large sliced onion, 3 cloves of garlic, and 2 sprigs each of fresh mint and coriander. Put this mixture through a very fine food chopper. Then add 2 beaten eggs and season with salt and pepper. Sift about 2 tablespoons of flour over the meat mixture for easy handling and mold into small balls. Drop the albondigas into 3 quarts of boiling soup stock which has been flavored with salt, pepper, and tomatoes. Cook this slowly for 1½ hours. Serve piping hot and see if your family won't ask for seconds once they have tasted this delicious soup.

The Latchstring Inn

THE dining room here is built on the edge of one of the most beautiful canyons in the Black Hills. Open for breakfast, lunch, and dinner from 7:00 a.m. to 10:00 p.m. Overnight accommodations and vacation facilities. Closed November 15 to May 1.

STRAWBERRY ICE-CREAM PIE

⅔ cup Eagle sweetened and condensed milk
½ cup water
1½ teaspoons vanilla
1 cup whipping cream
1 cup fresh or frozen strawberries
1 9-inch graham cracker crust

Mix milk, water, and vanilla. Chill in refrigerator; then fold in cream, whipped to consistency of custard. Freeze in freezing tray till mushy. Then put in bowl; beat till fluffy but not melted. Fold in berries; pour quickly into crust. Return to freezing compartment till ready to serve.

5

WEST
196

10 mi. s. of Spearfish on State 89, Savoy, S. D.

PAINTING BY EDGAR BRITTON

Grand Imperial Hotel   BUILT in 1882,

this historic hotel has been completely modernized and is one of the West's fine hostelries. Breakfast, lunch, and dinner served daily. Overnight and vacation facilities.

CHICKEN PANCAKES

8 5-inch crêpe suzette pancakes
12 ounces cooked chicken
1 cup sliced mushrooms combined with cream sauce and sherry wine
1 pint milk
4 eggs
Salt and pepper, to taste

Combine chicken with mushroom cream sauce and spread on pancakes. Roll pancakes and arrange in buttered oven-proof dish. Make a custard of milk, eggs, salt, and pepper. Pour custard over pancakes. Bake at 350° about 20 minutes, or till custard is done. Serve hot. Makes 4 portions.

Green Street, Silverton, Colorado

Parry Lodge

Parry Lodge IN the hub of the National Park area, this lodge is a favorite with tourists because of its true Western hospitality and its home-cooked meals. Open for breakfast, lunch, and dinner. Overnight accommodations and recreation facilities. Closed November 10 to May 1.

POT ROAST

5-pound beef roast
1 quart water
½ tablespoon mixed spices
1 tablespoon salt
1 tablespoon sugar
1 stalk celery, diced
2 onions, sliced
1 teaspoon pepper
½ teaspoon curry powder

Let roast stand in mixture of other ingredients 24 hours. Remove meat and sear in 425° oven for 20 minutes. Pour liquid over meat; cover and bake in 300° to 350° oven 2 or 3 hours, until tender. Remove meat. Mix 2 tablespoons melted butter and 2 of flour, and add to gravy. Cook gravy till thick. Strain and pour over meat. Serve with noodles or pineapple fritters.

U. S. 89, Kanab, Utah

WEST
198

Noble Hotel THIS small-town hotel can boast the conveniences and service of a metropolitan establishment, plus exceptional food. Breakfast, lunch, and dinner served every day in Indian Grill. Overnight accommodations and recreation facilities.

WESTERN-STYLE STEAK

There are steaks and there are recipes; so combine the two below and you will have a steak dinner with a real Western tang.

Allow an 8-ounce round steak per person, cut thick. Roll steak in flour and brown both sides quickly in a pan with a little bacon grease. Remove from fire and sprinkle the bottom of the pan with chopped mushrooms,

onions, and carrots. Add the steak, cover with a rich soup stock, and simmer; turn frequently for 20 minutes. Remove the steak, and thicken and season its juice with a roux to a light consistency. Replace steak and simmer until tender.

Serve on browned rice; cover with sauce and place a crisp fried egg on top.

Third and Main Streets, Lander, Wyoming

PAINTING BY ARNOLD MESCHES

Newhouse Hotel CHEF Louis Capella has long been noted as "the man behind the food" at this hotel, and now his creations are adding to the enjoyment of the new Royal Room. Breakfast, lunch, and dinner served. Overnight accommodations.

BROILED SQUAB CHICKEN

2½-pound broiler
Wild rice, cooked
½ clove garlic
1 can chopped mushrooms
½ cup chopped parsley
1 quart brown sauce
Orange slice

Maraschino cherries

Bone broiler and stuff with wild rice. Bruise garlic, then add mushrooms, parsley, and brown sauce. Cover squab with this mixture and bake in hot oven for 25 minutes. Garnish with orange slice and maraschino cherries before serving.

5

WEST
200

Fourth and Main Streets, Salt Lake City, Utah

El Merendero THIS low, rambling, Spanish-type restaurant run by Marian Waggener is one of the most popular in the city. Lunch and dinner served. Reservations necessary during the tourist season.

CREME DE MENTHE SUNDAE

Peppermint flavoring or
crème de menthe
½ cup crushed pineapple
and juice
1 cup sugar
½ cup white corn syrup
1 cup water
Dash of salt
Few drops green coloring

Boil all the ingredients together—except flavoring — until pineapple is clear. Add a few drops of peppermint flavoring or crème de menthe and pour over vanilla ice cream. Garnish each dish with a sprig of mint. Or during the holiday season pop a maraschino cherry on top of the sundae for a gala red-and-green color combination. Ice cream lovers will be delighted with the unusual dessert. This recipe makes enough topping for 6 ample servings.

2702 North Campbell, Tucson, Arizona

WEST

5

Pink Pony   THIS restaurant with its interesting pink pony decorations is as Western in appearance and atmosphere as a bucking bronco. Lunch and dinner served daily from 11:00 a.m. to 1:00 a.m.

SHEPHERD'S PIE

2 cups cooked, chopped lamb, beef, or veal

2 cups mashed potatoes

2 cups gravy, seasoned with salt, ¼ teaspoon pepper, and 1 teaspoon onion juice

¼ teaspoon paprika

2 tablespoons butter

Line bottom of a buttered baking dish or individual casseroles with hot mashed potatoes. Add thick layer of meat and seasoned gravy, then another layer of potato until dish is filled. Make top crust of potatoes. Dot with butter and sprinkle with paprika. Bake in hot oven until a golden brown.

Hacienda Dining Rooms IN the beautiful old 1706 home of one of the first governors of New Mexico, this spot reminds you of the color and glamor of the Spanish Conquistadores. Lunch and dinner served every day.

CALDO DE FRIJOLES (Mexican Bean Soup)

1 cup frijoles (pinto beans)
1 cup cold water, beef, or chicken broth
Seasonings: 2 green onions with tops, chopped; 1 clove garlic; 5 sprigs chopped parsley; 1 tablespoon chopped green chile; pulp of 1 red hot chile pepper (or 1½ teaspoons chile powder) ; 1 teaspoon oregano; ½ teaspoon salt
1 cup beef broth

Wash frijoles and soak overnight in cold water. Drain, add to quart of water or broth. Simmer 4 to 6 hours (adding boiling water as needed) till beans are tender. Add seasonings; simmer till tender. Then rub soup through colander and reheat. Add cup beef broth if necessary (soup should be consistency of thin purée). Serve with small rounds of toast, rolled in finely grated sharp cheese. This recipe serves 6 to 8.

Old Town Plaza, Old Albuquerque, New Mexico

El Tovar Hotel

You just can't beat the scene you view from this dining room, which is perched on the south rim of Grand Canyon. Breakfast, lunch, and dinner served. Overnight accommodations and vacation facilities.

BEEF TENDERLOIN—STROGANOFF

2 pounds tenderloin tips
1 medium-size onion, chopped
½ pound mushrooms
½ clove garlic
1 cup white wine
1 cup sour cream
Salt, pepper, and cayenne

Cut tenderloin tips in 2-inch slices about ⅜ inch thick; sauté with chopped onion over a high heat. Sauté mushrooms separately, adding garlic at the last minute. Mix all ingredients together. Simmer 5 minutes, season, and serve.

5

WEST

State Highway 64, Grand Canyon, Arizona

PAINTING BY REX BRANDT

Holiday House ALONG with delicious meals here there is a stunning view of sapphire-blue La Jolla Bay. Lunch and dinner served every day except Monday and Tuesday. Reservations necessary.

BROWN BREAD

1 cup flour
½ teaspoon baking powder
½ teaspoon baking soda
½ teaspoon salt
⅓ cup yellow corn meal
⅔ cup whole wheat flour
½ cup brown sugar (packed)
⅔ cup raisins
⅓ cup molasses
1⅓ cups buttermilk

Sift flour, baking powder, baking soda, and salt together. Crumble and add corn meal, wheat flour, brown sugar, raisins, and molasses. Blend in buttermilk, mix well, and pour into greased bread tin. Bake 2 to 2½ hours (until bread springs back to touch). Turn on side and let cool before turning out.

1270 Prospect Street, La Jolla, California

The Town House

THE Garden Room, with open terrace, is gay and attractive for dining and dancing. Lunch and dinner served from noon to 2:30 a.m. Overnight accommodations and vacation facilities.

CHICKEN PAGO-PAGO

Cut off the top of a whole coconut with a saw. Save the coconut milk. Wash inside thoroughly. Take half of a 2-pound chicken and fry in butter until done. Have ready some cooked wild rice, cooked fresh peas, and cooked chopped carrots in butter. Place wild rice in bottom of coconut, then peas and carrots. After removing all bone, cut fried chicken in small pieces. Place chicken back in frying pan with a little butter and ½ cup coconut milk; let simmer until almost dry. Place morsels of chicken inside coconut over cooked vegetables; season with curry powder, if desired; pour ½ cup coconut milk all over inside of coconut; and put the cut-off top of coconut in place.

Place coconut in a pan with hot water in bottom and cook in medium oven ½ hour.

2961 Wilshire Boulevard, Los Angeles, California

Hotel Bel-Air THE hotel is a series of rambling one-story buildings opening onto flowering patios. The expert cook is Chef Linassier. Breakfast, lunch, and dinner; overnight accommodations and recreation facilities.

PEAR BEL-AIR

    4 pears, cooked
    1 cup strawberries
    ⅓ cup sugar
        Dash vanilla extract
    1 quart cream, whipped
    1 pint English cream (below)

Mash fresh strawberries and add sugar, vanilla, whipped cream, and English cream. Place in freezer until solid. To serve, place strawberries in deep dish, follow with pear halves, and cover with Sabayon (below).

ENGLISH CREAM

Mix 3 egg yolks, ¼ cup sugar, and ½ cup sherry and cook till boiling point is reached, stirring constantly. Cool before using.

SABAYON

Whip 3 egg yolks, ¼ cup sugar, and ¾ cup milk together in double boiler till fluffy.

701 Stone Canyon Road, Los Angeles, California

La Avenida Café

GUESTS are attracted here from all over the country by the fine food and the priceless wall-length murals by the late Ramos Martínez. Lunch and dinner served every day except Monday. Reservations advisable.

ROMAINE SALAD

3 to 4 heads romaine, cut and chilled
2 handfuls crisp croutons
6 tablespoons garlic oil
    Salt to taste
    Black pepper
1 tablespoon Lea and Perrins sauce
2 ounces olive oil
6 ounces salad oil
6 heaping tablespoons freshly grated Romanello cheese
1 egg
    Juice of 3 lemons

Arrange the ingredients (all but egg and lemon juice) in salad bowl in order listed. Break egg over salad and pour lemon juice over egg. Toss salad from bottom. With salad serve garlic toast.

1301 Orange Avenue, Coronado, California

Irons' Cottage by the Sea

GUESTS at this seaside spot have a choice of eight or nine unusual salads with every meal. Open for lunch and dinner every day except Tuesday and Wednesday. Closed during February.

WHITE SALAD

4 egg yolks, beaten and slightly sweetened
1 cup milk
1 tablespoon gelatin
1 pint cream, whipped
1 No. 2½ can pineapple, crushed or in chunks
1 No. 2½ can white cherries, seeded and halved
¾ pound marshmallows, cut

Juice of 1 lemon
½ pound chopped blanched almonds

Mix beaten egg yolks with milk and scald in a double boiler. Soak gelatin in water to moisten and add to mixture. Fold in whipped cream and remaining ingredients. Let stand 24 hours in cool place. Garnish with lettuce. Serves 20.

501 Esplanade, Redondo Beach, California

Padua Hills Dining Room THE Institute,

a non-profit organization, encourages interest in the early culture of the region. It includes theatre and restaurant. Lunch and dinner except Monday and last two weeks in September.

BUNUELOS

4 eggs
½ cup milk
¼ cup melted butter or oleo
3 cups sifted flour
1 tablespoon sugar
1 teaspoon salt
  Oil or shortening for deep-frying
  Sugar
  Cinnamon

Beat eggs; add milk and melted butter. Sift dry ingredients into this to make a soft dough easily handled without sticking. Make into walnut-size balls; roll on slightly floured board into a large circle like a tortilla or very thin pancake. Fry in deep fat until golden brown. Drain and sprinkle with sugar mixed with ground stick cinnamon. At Christmas serve buñuelos broken into a soup bowl covered with thin syrup made by boiling 2 cups brown sugar in 2 cups water flavored with 1 stick cinnamon and 1 whole clove.

Padua Hills, Claremont, California

5

WEST

Café Caliente   BUILT on the site of the first winery in California, this café is famous for its Spanish food. Try their enchiladas, tacos, or chili. Open for lunch and dinner noon to 2:00 a.m. every day except Tuesday.

ARROZ CON POLLO A LA ESPANOLA EN CASSEROLE

2 strips bacon, squared
  Small piece of Chorizo
  (Mexican sausage)
2 broilers, jointed
2 cups rice
1 pimento, cut in small squares
¼ cup cooked peas
  Pinch of Spanish saffron
  Salt to taste

Fry bacon and Chorizo in a casserole until brown. Add chicken and rice and braise for 5 minutes. Add pimento, peas, saffron, and enough water to cover above ingredients by ½ inch. Cover and cook in 400° oven for 25 minutes. Spanish dishes are best when served piping hot.

20 Olvera Street, Los Angeles, California

PAINTING BY RALPH HULETT

Tail o' the Cock A FAVORITE nook here is the garden dining room—roofed to protect diners from California's "heavy dew." Lunch, dinner daily, 11:30 a.m. to 2:00 a.m.

BARBECUED BRISKET OF FRESH BEEF

8 to 10 pounds fresh brisket beef
8 ounces Milani's barbecue sauce
1 quart catsup
6 ounces wine vinegar
3 ounces Lea and Perrins sauce
2 tablespoons liquid smoke
2 tablespoons prepared mustard
3 tablespoons fresh lime juice
6 bay leaves
1 clove garlic, crushed
12 whole peppercorns
1 cup consommé, if necessary

Wipe beef dry, trim, and rub with salt. Prepare sauce by combining remaining ingredients.

Place beef in heavy pan, pour the sauce over it, and cook for 3½ hours in a preheated oven at 350°. Turn and baste every half hour. If sauce becomes too thick, add a cupful of consommé. Serve with purée of split peas.

477 South La Cienega, Los Angeles, California

Mattei's Tavern THIS establishment, surrounded by rolling hills and canyons, was built in 1886 by the father of the present owner and has been in continuous operation by a member of the family ever since. Breakfast, lunch, and dinner served. Overnight accommodations.

SPECIAL SALAD

- 3 heads lettuce
- 6 hard-boiled eggs
- 3 stalks celery
- 1 medium-size onion
- ½ cup mayonnaise
- 1 tablespoon lemon juice

Coarse-ground black pepper and salt to taste

Shred lettuce and chop hard-boiled eggs, celery, and onion. Combine ingredients and mix thoroughly. This recipe makes a generous and nourishing serving for 8 to 10 persons.

3 miles east of U.S. 101, Los Olivos, California

Don the Beachcomber

THIS popular eating place is distinguished by its original South Sea Island atmosphere, complete with decorations of sharks' jaws, turtle shells, and native art work. Dinner served from 5:00 p.m. to 1:00 a.m. every day except Thanksgiving and Christmas. Reservations necessary.

BEACHCOMBER CANTONESE SPARERIBS

2 sides pork spareribs
2 cups Chinese soya sauce
1 cup sugar
2 teaspoons salt
2 tablespoons catsup

Trim ribs and marinate for an hour in mixture of soya sauce, sugar, salt, and catsup. Roast in 400° oven for approximately 30 minutes. Baste at least 3 times. Roasting time will vary with thickness of ribs. Serve with barbecue sauce.

This is a recipe ideal for an outdoor barbecue.

5

WEST
214

1727 North McCadden Place, Hollywood, California

PAINTING BY RALPH HULETT

The Brown Derby

THIS is one of Hollywood's most famous restaurants. It is presided over by Montana-bred Bob Cobb. Open 24 hours; breakfast, lunch, and dinner served. Reservations necessary.

HAMBURGER DE LUXE

- 2 pounds ground sirloin
- 1 raw egg
- 2 cups chicken broth
- ½ teaspoon English mustard
- 1 tablespoon salt
- 1 teaspoon black pepper
- 2 tablespoons Worcestershire
- 2 teaspoons chicken fat

Mix meat, egg, and broth, then add the other ingredients. Use one full coffee cup of the mixture for each portion. Serve with braised onions or De Luxe sauce. (To make this sauce combine: 2 cups brown sauce, either canned or from a beef roast; 1 tablespoon English mustard, 2 teaspoons Sauce Diable or A-1 sauce, 1 tablespoon Worcestershire sauce, ½ cup catsup, 2 pats butter. Boil together, adding a little parsley.) Pour over hamburgers.

1628 North Vine Street, Hollywood, California

The Harbor Restaurant LOCATED on the end of a dock overlooking the Pacific Ocean, this restaurant just naturally specializes in sea food. Open for dinner from 5:00 p.m. to 11:00 p.m. on weekdays, and from 1:00 p.m. to 10:00 p.m. on Sunday. Reservations necessary.

ABALONE BEURRE NOIR

4 slices white abalone
  Flour
1 egg
2 ounces butter
  Juice of ½ lemon
1 tablespoon capers

Season abalone, roll in flour, and dip in beaten egg. Fry in skillet with a little oil over rapid flame (about 2 minutes on each side—until golden brown). Cook butter until brown, then add lemon juice and capers. Pour over abalone and serve.

At the foot of State Street, Santa Barbara, California

PAINTING BY RALPH HULETT

Cold Spring Tavern

ONCE a stage stop, this restaurant now has a three-ton trout aquarium in the main dining room. Open for lunch and dinner from noon until 9:00 p.m. daily. Closed November through April.

MONTE CARLO SANDWICH

Break large egg in a bowl; add 2 tablespoons cream. Blend with a 2-tined cooking fork. DO NOT BEAT TOO MUCH. Take 2 slices white bread and trim crusts. Butter both slices. On one piece of buttered bread, put a layer of sliced breast of chicken, a slice of baked ham, and a slice of brick cheese. Top with the other bread slice, and halve diagonally. Toothpick each side to hold together, and dip into beater egg and cream.

Grease an ordinary pancake griddle with oil and let it get hot. Cook sandwich on both sides and all edges until golden brown.

Serve with cold potato salad.

State Highway 150, Santa Barbara, California

Cliff House In the dining room here you have a ring-side seat near the famed Seal Rocks, where hundreds of sea lions frolic in the blue waters of the Golden Gate. Breakfast, lunch, and dinner served from 9:00 a.m. to 10:00 p.m., week-days; Sundays, from 10:00 a.m. to 8:30 p.m., except Monday during winter.

CRABMEAT MONZA

Meat of 1 large crab
1 pound large mushrooms
2 ounces butter
Salt and pepper
1 teaspoon Worcestershire sauce
2 heads shallots
2 ounces sherry
3 level tablespoons flour

1 cup table cream
Grated cheese

Quarter mushrooms and simmer in butter for 30 minutes. Add crabmeat, seasonings, and cream-and-flour mixture. Cook until sauce is smooth. Fill individual shells, sprinkle grated cheese on top, and bake for 5 minutes.

5

WEST
218

Great Highway at Seal Rocks, San Francisco, California

The Palace Hotel

THIS elegant hotel's most impressive dining room is the Garden Court. Ionic marble columns support the high-vaulted glass dome from which the magnificent chandeliers hang. Breakfast, lunch, dinner, and snacks to midnight. Overnight accommodations.

QUICHE LORRAINE

Line a regulation-size pie tin with a flaky-type crust. Do not bake. Cover with a layer of diced ham or diced half-cooked bacon. Put on a layer of Swiss cheese shavings. In a separate bowl prepare a custard mix of:

4 whole eggs and 2 yolks
1 quart homogenized milk
   or light cream
Dash of salt, pepper, and nutmeg

Beat eggs until light and creamy. Add milk and spices, then stir thoroughly. Pour mixture over ham and cheese in the half-filled pie tin, bringing liquid level to edge of pastry. Bake 25 minutes in a slow oven (250°), or until custard is firm and golden brown. Will serve 4 to 6 as a main dish, or up to 12 as an extra. Plan it for a party menu over the holiday.

Market and New Montgomery Streets, San Francisco, California

WEST

5

Andersen's Pea Soup Restaurant

YEARS ago Anton Andersen made split-pea soup his specialty. Today his son Robert uses over a carload of peas a year to serve over 200,000 dishes of the delectable soup. Continuous service from 7:00 a.m. to 9:00 p.m.

SPLIT PEA SOUP

2 quarts soft water
2 cups Andersen's Special Idaho green split peas
1 stalk celery, chopped
1 large carrot, chopped
1 small onion, chopped
¼ teaspoon thyme
1 pinch cayenne pepper
1 bay leaf
Salt and pepper

Boil ingredients vigorously for 20 minutes, then slowly until the peas are done. Strain this mixture through a colander. This recipe will make 8 servings of a soup that is noted all over California for its excellence. If you are a connoisseur of soups, you will make a meal of this one.

U.S. 101, Buellton, California

5

Colonial House IT would be hard to pass this restaurant with its grinning chef in front, waving diners inside with a flourish of his carving knife. Lunch and dinner served daily. Entertainment nightly in the Copper Room.

CALIFORNIA AVOCADO STUFFED WITH SHRIMP

Select 2 medium-sized avocados, soft but not overripe. Cut in half lengthwise, remove seed, and peel. Lay each half on a bed of shredded lettuce in a cup of lettuce leaves. Fill with Shrimp Mixture.

SHRIMP MIXTURE

Combine 1 cup chopped shrimp with ½ cup chopped celery and 2 hard-boiled eggs, also chopped. Bind with mayonnaise. Place this mixture on avocado halves and top with a dab of mayonnaise. Garnish salad plate with hard-boiled egg slices, lemon quarters, stuffed olives. Makes a typical California luncheon dish for 4.

PAINTING BY JAMES LAWRENCE

The Nut Tree MANY have tried to pry recipes from the secretive chef here, but to date we alone have been successful. The restaurant is famous for its salads, homemade bread, and chocolate fudge cake. Breakfast, lunch, and dinner served to 9:00 p.m.

MARSHMALLOW DRESSING

5 ounces light Karo syrup
1 cup sugar
½ cup hot water
2 egg whites
Vanilla to taste
⅓ cup mayonnaise
Orange rind, grated

Combine syrup, sugar, and hot water, and cook until mixture registers 248° or will form a thread. Beat egg whites stiff; then add hot sugar syrup slowly to eggs while continuing to beat. Flavor with vanilla. When cool, add mayonnaise and orange rind, and serve with your favorite fruit salad. For a dessert, spread marshmallow dressing over a slice of orange nut bread and top with strawberries.

WEST

U.S. 40, Vacaville, California

Locatelli's Inn FOR over 30 years this restaurant run by Catherine Locatelli has been noted for its fine Italian food. Lunch and dinner served every day until 2:00 a.m., June through August; closed Thursdays rest of year. Closed December 10 through 28. Overnight accommodations.

CHEESE SPREAD

1 pound Roquefort or blue cheese
5 tablespoons lemon juice
5 tablespoons Worcestershire sauce
2 tablespoons A-1 sauce
1 teaspoon dry mustard
1 teaspoon pepper
4 cakes Philadelphia cream cheese
  or 1 pound cottage cheese

Cut Roquefort cheese in small pieces. Place in electric mixer bowl. Add lemon juice, sauces, mustard, and pepper. Beat, using low speed, till light and smooth. Add cottage or cream cheese. Beat again to the consistency of heavy whipped cream. This spread can be kept for weeks in the refrigerator in a tightly covered jar.

Big Basin Highway, Boulder Creek, California

WEST 5

Trader Vic's PREPARE yourself for some exciting food accompanied by exotic rum drinks afloat with gardenias. The bamboo-lined dining room is decorated with curios from the South Pacific. Dinner served from 4:30 p.m. to 1:00 a.m. except Christmas Day and Thanksgiving Day. Reservations.

STEAK HAWAIIAN

Chop a clove of garlic very fine and put it in a large, shallow, glass baking dish or platter. Add ½ to 1 cup soya sauce and mix. Marinate your steak in this for 15 minutes, turning it thoroughly to flavor the meat with the seasoning and soak up the sauce. Then barbecue, fry, or broil the steak, as you prefer. This steak dish is cooked at Trader Vic's in a huge Chinese oven.

BARBECUED SQUAB

Brush whole squabs inside and out with soya sauce and barbecue 20 to 25 minutes. Or place in a hot oven and roast until done. Roasted squabs should be basted occasionally with a mixture of soya sauce and melted butter.

6500 San Pablo Avenue, Oakland, California

L'Omelette French Restaurant THIS

establishment run by André and Pierre Frelier specializes in such French delicacies as crêpe suzettes, snails, and onion soup. Dinner except Monday and Tuesday. Closed July 5 to 18.

OMELETTE AU RHUM

4 eggs
½ cup milk
½ ounce butter
Pinch of salt
Rum
Confectioner's sugar

Beat the eggs with the milk and add the salt. Heat the butter in the frying pan until it gives off the characteristic nutty smell. (This will not only lend an exquisite taste to the omelet but the degree of heat reached will insure a perfect setting for the eggs.) Pour in the beaten eggs and stir briskly with a fork to heat the whole mass evenly. When it is well set, roll up the omelet and transfer it to a hot dish; draw a piece of butter quickly across its surface to make it glossy. Sprinkle the omelet with confectioner's sugar and heated rum. Light the rum and bring it to the table.

4170 El Camino Real, Palo Alto, California

Cathay House

IN this Chinese restaurant, with black walls adorned with magnificent gold murals, guests look down over San Francisco's famous Chinatown. Lunch and dinner every day except Thanksgiving and Christmas Day. Reservations advisable.

BOR LOR PAI GWUT (Pineapple and Spareribs)

Cut spareribs into small bite-size pieces. Precook in deep oil and then allow all the oil to drain off. Replace in skillet with a little oil and add a little water. After allowing spareribs to simmer about 5 minutes, add several slices of pineapple which have been diced to about bite size.

Now proceed with the sweet and sour sauce as follows: make a thickening out of cornstarch and water. Add a good wine vinegar and sugar to suit the individual taste. Consistency of this thickening should be heavy. Add to the spareribs, bring to a slight simmer, then serve.

718 California Street, San Francisco, California

Trinity Alps Resort THIS restaurant spans

Stuart's Fork of the Trinity River, enabling diners to view the rushing stream and the fish below. Breakfast, lunch, and dinner served. Overnight and vacation facilities. Closed October 15 to April 30. Reservations necessary.

SWISS STEAK TRINITY ALPS

4-pound round steak (in serving pieces)
⅔ cup flour
4 tablespoons shortening
1 large onion, sliced
2 teaspoons salt
Pepper to taste
2 bay leaves
½ teaspoon Beau Monde seasoning
1 large can tomatoes

Roll the meat in flour, pounding in as much of the flour as possible with a meat pounder. Place shortening in a heavy skillet and heat well. Add meat and brown on both sides, then add 2 cups water, onion, and seasoning. Simmer slowly for about 2 hours, adding water as necessary. Just before removing the steak from the fire, cover with tomatoes and simmer a few seconds longer.

15 mi. west of Redding off U.S. 299, Lewiston, California

Fishermen's Grotto You dine over the Bay in the second-floor dining room here and command a view of the ever-bustling activity of the fishing smacks. Lunch and dinner served from 10:00 a.m. until 2:00 a.m.

SPAGHETTI AND CRAB, FISHERMAN STYLE

1 pound spaghetti
1 pound fresh or canned crab meat
½ cup chopped onions
1 teaspoon chopped celery
1 teaspoon chopped garlic
1 teaspoon chopped parsley
¼ cup olive oil
1 cup solid-pack tomatoes
1 cup tomato sauce
1½ cups water
1 teaspoon black pepper
2 teaspoonfuls salt
½ teaspoon paprika
¼ cup sherry
Grated cheese

Braise onions, celery, garlic, and parsley in oil until golden brown. Add tomatoes, tomato sauce, water, and seasonings. Simmer for 1 hour. Add crab meat and wine and simmer a few minutes. Cook spaghetti. Drain but do not wash. Add to sauce. Mix well. Pour on platter and sprinkle with grated cheese.

Number 9 Fishermen's Wharf, San Francisco, California

Camlin Hotel THE Cloud Room on the top of this hotel is noted for its splendid native sea food. Breakfast, lunch, and dinner. Overnight accommodations. Reservations necessary.

SALMON STEAK, CALCUTTA STYLE

Boneless salmon in slices about
    1½ inches thick
Salt and pepper
½ cup sherry
½ cup fish stock
Pepper oil

Put salmon slices in flat oiled pan. Season with salt and pepper. Add sherry and stock. Cover with pepper oil and cook in oven 20 minutes. Then put fish on platter and keep hot. Cover with following sauce.

Ninth and Pine, Seattle, Washington

SAUCE

1 shallot, chopped
1 teaspoon flour
1 teaspoon curry powder
  Broth from fish cooked above
1 pint fish stock
2 egg yolks
½ cup cream

Sauté shallot with flour and curry powder. Heat through. Add broth and fish stock. Boil 2 minutes. Blend with egg yolks and cream. Strain and pour over fish.

WEST 5

Oregon Caves Château ADJACENT to famous limestone caves, this student-staffed spot is well known for its food. A natural stream runs right through the building. Breakfast, lunch, and dinner 7:30 a.m. to 10:00 p.m. Overnight accommodations. Open May 29 to September 15.

ANGEL PIE

Beat 4 egg whites stiff; add ½ teaspoon cream of tartar and 1 cup sugar. Spread on a well-greased and -floured pie tin and bake 20 minutes in a 275° oven and 40 minutes at 300°.

FILLING

For half the filling, cook the following ingredients for 8 minutes in a double boiler:

    4 egg yolks
    ½ cup sugar (scant)

    1 tablespoon lemon juice
    2 tablespoons pineapple juice
    Rind of lemon, grated

For the other half of the filling whip together 1 cup whipping cream and 1 tablespoon sugar. Spread half of whipped cream on pie shell. Add lemon mixture and remaining whipped cream. Chill pie in refrigerator and serve.

Oregon Caves, Oregon

Manuel's LOCATED in the "Old Town" section of the city, this restaurant is open daily for lunch and dinner from 11:00 a.m. to 10:00 p.m. The adobe building and patio, built in 1838, are among California's historic landmarks.

TAMALE PIE

Stir ⅔ cup corn meal into 2 cups rapidly boiling water. Cook, stirring, till thick; then remove from stove. Melt 2 tablespoons margarine in heavy skillet; add 1 small chopped onion. When brown, add ½ pound ground beef. Cook mixture, stirring, till meat is no longer red. Then add 1 can tomato paste, ½ cup ripe olives, ¼ cup stuffed olives (sliced), ¼ cup green peppers (chopped), 1 teaspoon chili powder, ½ cup beef bouillon or consommé, ½ cup whole kernel corn, cayenne pepper and salt to taste. Stir well and taste for seasonings. Line a shallow baking dish with part of cornmeal mush. Pour in meat-and-vegetable mixture; cover with remaining mush. Top with ½ cup shredded cheese; sprinkle with paprika. Bake in 350° oven for 1 hour. Serves 6. Pie may be prepared in advance, even to cooking, and reheated in moderate oven before serving.

A block from U.S. 101, 80, at 2616 San Diego Avenue, San Diego, Calif. **WEST**
231

Ruby Chow's Chinese Dinner Club

THIS is one of the few restaurants in the country that refuse to indulge the American palate with such artificial Chinese food as chop suey. It has all native food cooked by native Chinese. Dinner served from 6:00 p.m. to 2:00 a.m. (Sunday: 3:00 p.m. to 11:00 p.m.) Closed Monday. Reservations advisable.

MELON SOUP

1 pound Chinese melon
1 quart chicken stock
¼ pound raw pork, diced
3 Chinese water chestnuts, peeled
1 egg

Pour stock into a 2-quart saucepan and bring to a rapid boil. Add pork and sliced water chestnuts; cook until pork is done. Then add salt and melon, cut into bite size; boil 10 minutes. *Do not cover pan after adding melon.* Break egg into soup. *Do not stir*, as the egg is supposed to remain whole. Serve immediately. Some Chinese prefer to break egg into serving bowl, then pour hot soup onto raw egg.

Broadway and Jefferson Streets, Seattle, Washington

Lake Crescent Lodge

THE front lawn of this rustic resort drops off suddenly into the vivid blue of the lake for which it is named. Breakfast, lunch, and dinner. Overnight accommodations in main lodge or in cabins. Vacation facilities. Closed from Labor Day to Memorial Day.

SCHAUM TORTE

> 7 egg whites
> 2 cups sugar, sifted
> 1 teaspoon vanilla
> 1 tablespoon vinegar

Beat egg whites until stiff, but not dry. Continuing to beat, add sugar slowly, to make a meringue. When sugar is dissolved, add vanilla and vinegar. Drop meringue in desired pattern onto baking dish lined with brown paper. Bake in slow oven (300°) 1 hour. Cool. Remove from baking sheet with spatula. Break off top half of torte and fill with sweetened or unsweetened whipped cream and fresh or canned fruit. Makes 8 large tortes.

U.S. 101, 20 miles west of Port Angeles, Washington

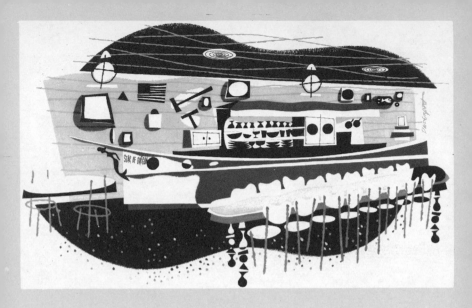

Dan Louis Oyster Bar   OWNER Louis

Wachsmuth began to serve oyster cocktails and stews in a little room next to his wholesale sea-food business. Today his restaurant serves more oysters than any other on the West Coast. Open for lunch and dinner from 11:00 a.m. to 1:00 a.m.

OYSTER STEW

1 pint oysters (Olympia or Yaquina) or 24 of Bluepoint size
2 quarts milk
½ pint cream
⅓ pound butter
1 teaspoon Schilling's Savor Salt
Salt and black pepper to taste

Heat milk and cream in double boiler until piping hot. Stirring constantly, add butter, salt, pepper, Schilling's Salt. Drop half of oysters into pot (to make stew), and simmer for at least 5 minutes. Taste for seasoning. Then drop remaining oysters into boiling water. When edges of oysters curl, remove from water, drain, and put in deep bowls. Stir stew again; then pour over oysters in bowls. Serve immediately with pat of butter. Makes enough stew for 6.

208 Southwest Ankeny Street, Portland, Oregon

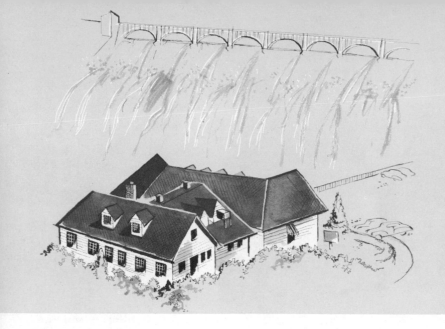

Green Hut THIS café, a stone's throw from the mighty Grand Coulee Dam, serves over a half million tourists yearly. A gift shop also is maintained. Open for breakfast, lunch, and dinner to 11:00 p.m.

BAKED HAM WITH BRANDY SAUCE

12- to 14-pound choice ham with
    short shank
    Cloves
    Brown sugar
    Honey
1 pint clear apple juice or cider

Soak ham overnight in cold water; drain, and re-cover with fresh cold water. Bring to a boil and simmer until tender (approximately 2½ hours). Remove rind and some of the fat. Make a series of cuts across the remaining fat, forming squares or diamonds about ½ inch in diameter. Put in roaster, stud with cloves, and cover with brown sugar and honey. Add apple juice or cider. Glaze in a hot oven, basting frequently. Serve with:

BRANDY SAUCE
    Bring to a boil:
    1 quart apple cider or juice
    1 pound brown sugar
    6 cloves
    Juice of 2 oranges

Remove from the stove and add 2 ounces brandy.

State Highway 2, Coulee Dam, Washington

Dupuis Tavern FRIENDLY Mrs. Karl Kirk greets guests at this restaurant, dramatically set among tall firs and facing mountains of the Olympic group. Lunch and dinner, 10:00 a.m. to 10:00 p.m., in the cedar-paneled dining room.

PINK SAUCE FOR CRAB

    1 cup mayonnaise
    1 cup chili sauce
    1 teaspoon Worcestershire sauce
    2 teaspoons horseradish
    4 sweet pickles, chopped fine
    2 stalks celery
    4 green onions
    4 sprigs parsley
    1 tablespoon sugar

Mix all ingredients together and serve over crab.

ROQUEFORT CHEESE SPREAD

    ½ pound Roquefort cheese
    4 small packages Philadelphia
      cream cheese
    Port (enough wine to form paste)

Blend ingredients and chill thoroughly. Serve with toasted crackers and strawberry jam.

This is a traditional dessert here after a sea-food dinner.

5

WEST

236

U.S. 101, Port Angeles, Washington

Shamrock Inn

MARY McCRANK describes her restaurant as "home-by-the-side-of-the-road" and lives up to her boast by serving fresh fruits, vegetables, and homemade bread. Open for lunch and dinner every day except holidays. Open Thanksgiving Day.

FRUIT SALAD DRESSING

1 cup pineapple juice
1 cup orange juice
½ cup lemon juice
1½ cups sugar
4 egg yolks
2 heaping tablespoons cornstarch
2 tablespoons butter

Mix juices with sugar in top of double boiler. When hot, add egg yolks, slightly beaten and blended with cornstarch. Cook 15 to 20 minutes; stir in butter after removing from stove. Dressing may be served plain or folded into whipped cream for fruit salad topping.

U.S. 99, Chehalis, Washington

Maison Blanc ONE of the state's oldest restaurants, this establishment has long been noted for its international cuisine. Open for lunch and dinner 11:30 a.m. to midnight, except Sunday.

ONION SOUP A LA BLANC

    4 large white onions
    ¼ pound butter
    2 ounces flour
    1 quart chicken broth
    1 quart water
      Salt and pepper
      Dry French bread, toasted
      Swiss or Parmesan cheese,
        grated
Cut onions in thin slices and fry slowly in butter until lightly browned. Sprinkle with flour. Add chicken broth, water, salt, and pepper. Boil 10 minutes. Cut French bread in thin slices and toast. Pour soup in individual containers, ⅔ full, and cover with a layer of toasted bread and grated cheese. Add more soup, repeat toast and cheese. Top with butter squares and bake in hot oven until golden brown.

306-308 Marion Street, Seattle, Washington

Beau Brummel ABOUT 80 dishes are featured on the huge smorgasbord, as well as French and Danish pastries. Open lunch and dinner 11:30 a.m. to 10:00 p.m.; smorgasbord Wednesday through Sunday. Reservations advisable.

VERMLANDS FLÄSK KÖRV (SWEDISH PORK SAUSAGE)

2 pounds pork shoulder
½ pound veal shoulder
1½ pounds cold boiled potatoes
2 tablespoons salt
¾ tablespoon sugar
¼ tablespoon each of white pepper, ginger, and ground cloves
Pinch of saltpeter
1¾ quarts milk
Hog casing

Grind meat in fine grinder twice. Grind potatoes; mix with meat. Add condiments. Add milk slowly, mixing till smooth. Stuff loosely in casing. *For brine:* combine 2½ cups water, 1 lb. sugar, 1 lb. salt, 1 teaspoon saltpeter. Bring to a boil; chill. Coil sausage in a crock, cover with brine, and leave in refrigerator 2 weeks. *To cook sausage:* place in cold water with bay leaf and allspice. Cook 20 to 30 minutes.

3100 Highland Drive, Salt Lake City, Utah

PAINTING BY HARRY BONATH

The Crabapple A SPECIAL feature of this delightful spot is the crabapple jelly and spiced crabapple that comes with all meals. Lunch and dinner served weekdays noon to midnight; Sunday and holidays 4:00 p.m. to 9:00 p.m. Closed Mondays and most holidays. Reservations advisable.

DUTCH OVEN STEAK

2 pounds round steak, 1 inch thick
1 cup flour
1 tablespoon salt
1 teaspoon black pepper
½ cup shortening
1 large onion, chopped fine
1 can mushroom soup

Pound steak with tenderizer. Pour flour into shallow pan; add salt and pepper. Press steak into flour mixture and turn several times. Melt shortening in heated Dutch oven (425°). Brown steak well on both sides, then add chopped onion. Mix mushroom soup with equal parts of water, stir well, and pour over steak. Turn fire down to 350° and let simmer for 2 hours. Add more water if necessary. Serves 4 to 6.

King Oscar's Smörgasbord

IN this former estate home of a Danish sea captain William Jensen, owner and host, has created a relaxing atmosphere. Dinner every day except Monday.

SWEDISH PANCAKES

    4 eggs
    2 cups milk
    ½ cup flour
    ½ teaspoon salt
    2 tablespoons sugar

Add all ingredients together and beat until smooth. Bake on moderately hot grill, spreading batter as thin as possible. When golden brown, spread with jelly or jam and roll off grill. Sprinkle with powdered sugar before serving.

4312 Aurora Avenue, Seattle, Washington

ROLLED SMELTS

    2 pounds smelts, boned and
        cleaned
    3 cups water
    1 cup vinegar
    ½ cup sugar
    2 bay leaves
    10 whole allspice

Roll smelts up lengthwise and secure with toothpicks. Mix other ingredients and bring to boil. Put in the smelts and boil 2 minutes. Cool smelts in brine before serving.

PAINTING BY JAMES M. BOYLE

Trail Coffee Shop IN a true Western town, famous for its Frontier Days' celebration, this dining room is a friendly place to stop for good food. Open for breakfast, lunch, and dinner from 6:00 a.m. to 1:00 a.m. daily.

SOUR CREAM RAISIN PIE

1 cup raisins
1 cup sugar
1 cup water
  Pinch of salt
2 tablespoons flour
2 egg yolks, well beaten
1 cup sour cream
1 teaspoon vanilla
1 9-inch pie shell, unbaked

English walnuts
Meringue

Cook raisins, sugar, water, and salt over slow heat till quite thick. Cool; then stir in flour, egg yolks, cream, and vanilla. Pour mixture into pie shell and sprinkle top with walnuts. Bake at 400° for 20 minutes; then at 350° till filling is firm (about 40 to 45 minutes). Cool pie; then top with meringue and brown in slow oven.

5

WEST
242

216 West 16th Street (U.S. 30), Cheyenne, Wyoming

PAINTING BY BEN NORRIS

The Willows An exotic tropical garden surrounds this restaurant, which was once a private estate. The dining room is a thatched-roofed pavilion overlooking a flowering lagoon. Lunch and dinner served every day except Sunday.

HAWAIIAN CHICKEN

Cut 3- or 4-pound chicken for fricassee and simmer until tender. Add 1 quart washed spinach and Cream of Coconut (see below). Simmer for ½ hour. Add salt to taste.

CREAM OF COCONUT

Add 1 cup boiling water or milk to grated meat of 2 coconuts. Allow to stand for an hour and squeeze through cheesecloth.

901 Hausten Street, Honolulu, Hawaii

Don the Beachcomber   MAINTAINING a

tradition he started in his first two establishments in Los Angeles and Chicago, Don features exotic rum drinks and succulent South Sea feasts. Dinner until 1:00 a.m. daily. Native feast with entertainment Sunday. Reservations necessary.

CHINESE-HAWAIIAN BARBECUED RIBS

1 inch of green ginger root
½ clove garlic
½ cup soya sauce
¾ cup sugar
½ cup catsup
2 ounces sherry
1 teaspoon salt

Crush ginger root and garlic. Place in pan. Blend remaining ingredients into a sauce. Rub it into a section of young pork loin back ribs and marinate for 3 hours. Place ribs on rack in a 325° oven and cook ¾ hour. Place a shallow pan of water under ribs to catch falling juices. Use balance of sauce for basting. Remove from oven, cut up each rib, and serve hot as a delectable appetizer.

Waikiki Beach, Honolulu, Hawaii

Canlis' Charcoal Broiler

HERE at a wonderful open-faced charcoal grill the chef stands deftly turning choice cuts of island fish and flown-in delicacies. These in turn are served by Japanese girls garbed in traditional kimonos. Open for dinner. Reservations necessary.

FRIED JUMBO SHRIMP—CANLIS

Shell and clean uncooked jumbo shrimp, leaving tail section intact. Allow 9 or 10 per person. Cover the bottom of a deep skillet with imported olive oil and heat until piping hot. Place enough shrimp in the pan to cover the bottom. Cook until golden brown (about 7 minutes), turning constantly. Before shrimp are completely cooked, sprinkle with salt and freshly ground pepper (when you think you've seasoned sufficiently, add more). Turn fire down low, and saturate with dry vermouth, juice of a whole lemon, and 2 pats of butter. Allow to simmer for 5 minutes. Serve at once.

2100 Kalakaua Avenue, Honolulu, Hawaii

Index

Alphabetical Index of Recipes

The United States

TRAVELER'S KEY TO REGIONAL
DIVISIONS COVERED BY THIS
GUIDE TO INTERESTING
EATING PLACES